WE SHALL FIGHT UNTIL WE WIN

A CENTURY OF PIONEERING POLITICAL WOMEN.
THE GRAPHIC ANTHOLOGY.

@404ink

@BHP_Comics

www.WeShallFightUntilWeWin.com

Edited by: Laura Jones, Heather McDaid and
Sha Nazir

Publication design by: Kirsty Hunter

Back Cover illustration by: Charlot Kristensen

Special Thanks: Nyla Ahmed and Heather Palmer

First printing 2018

Published in Glasgow by BHP Comics Ltd and
404 Ink Ltd

ISBN: 978-1-910775-16-5

Made in Scotland. Printed in Great Britain byBell
& Bain Ltd, Glasgow

A CIP catalogue reference for this book is
available from the British Library

Ask your local comic or bookshop to stock
BHP Comics and 404 Ink.

Visit www.WeShallFightUntilWeWin.com
for more info.

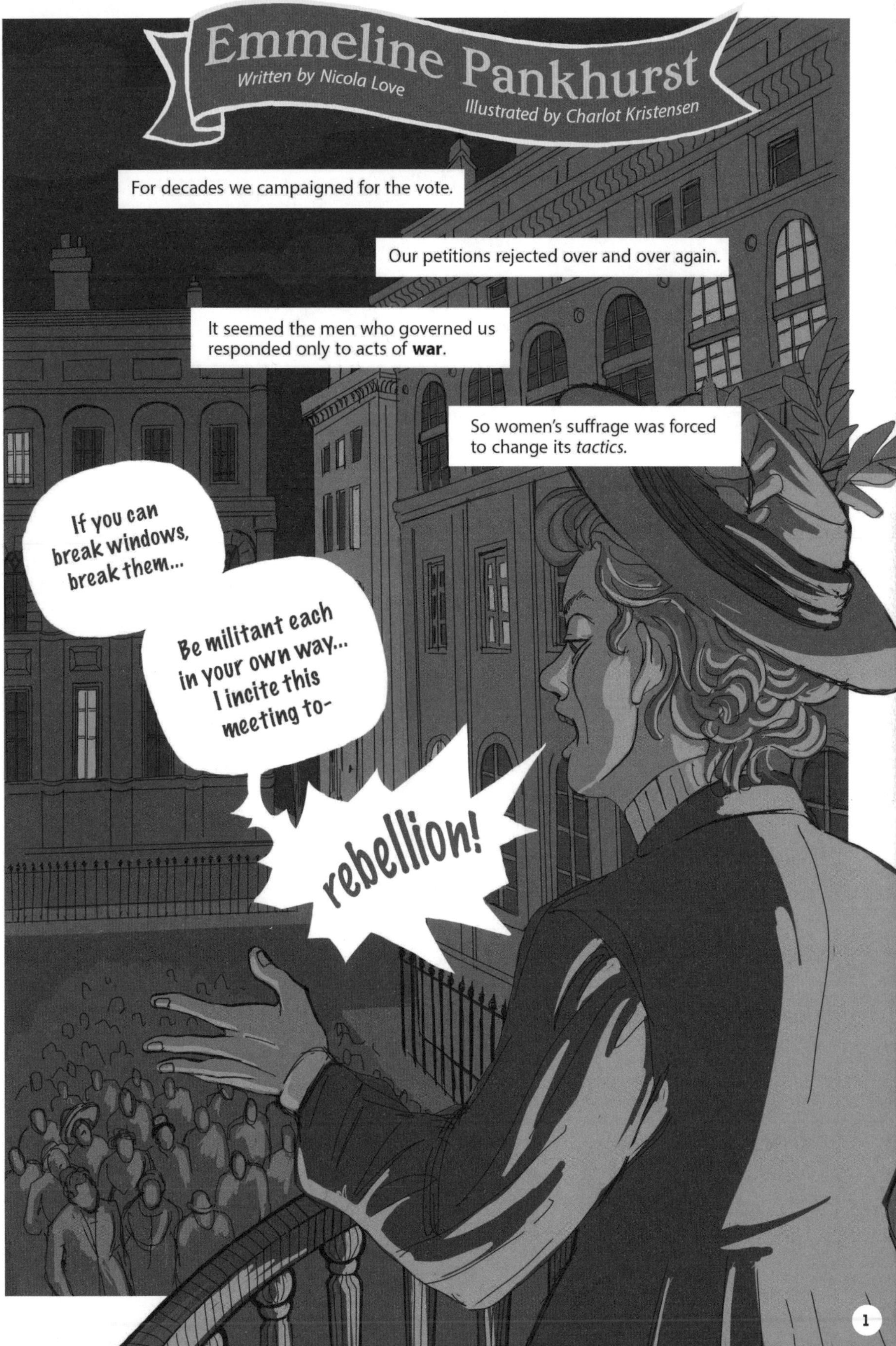
Emmeline Pankhurst
Written by Nicola Love
Illustrated by Charlot Kristensen
For decades we campaigned for the vote.
Our petitions rejected over and over again.
It seemed the men who governed us responded only to acts of **war**.
So women's suffrage was forced to change its *tactics*.
If you can break windows, break them...
Be militant each in your own way... I incite this meeting to-
rebellion!

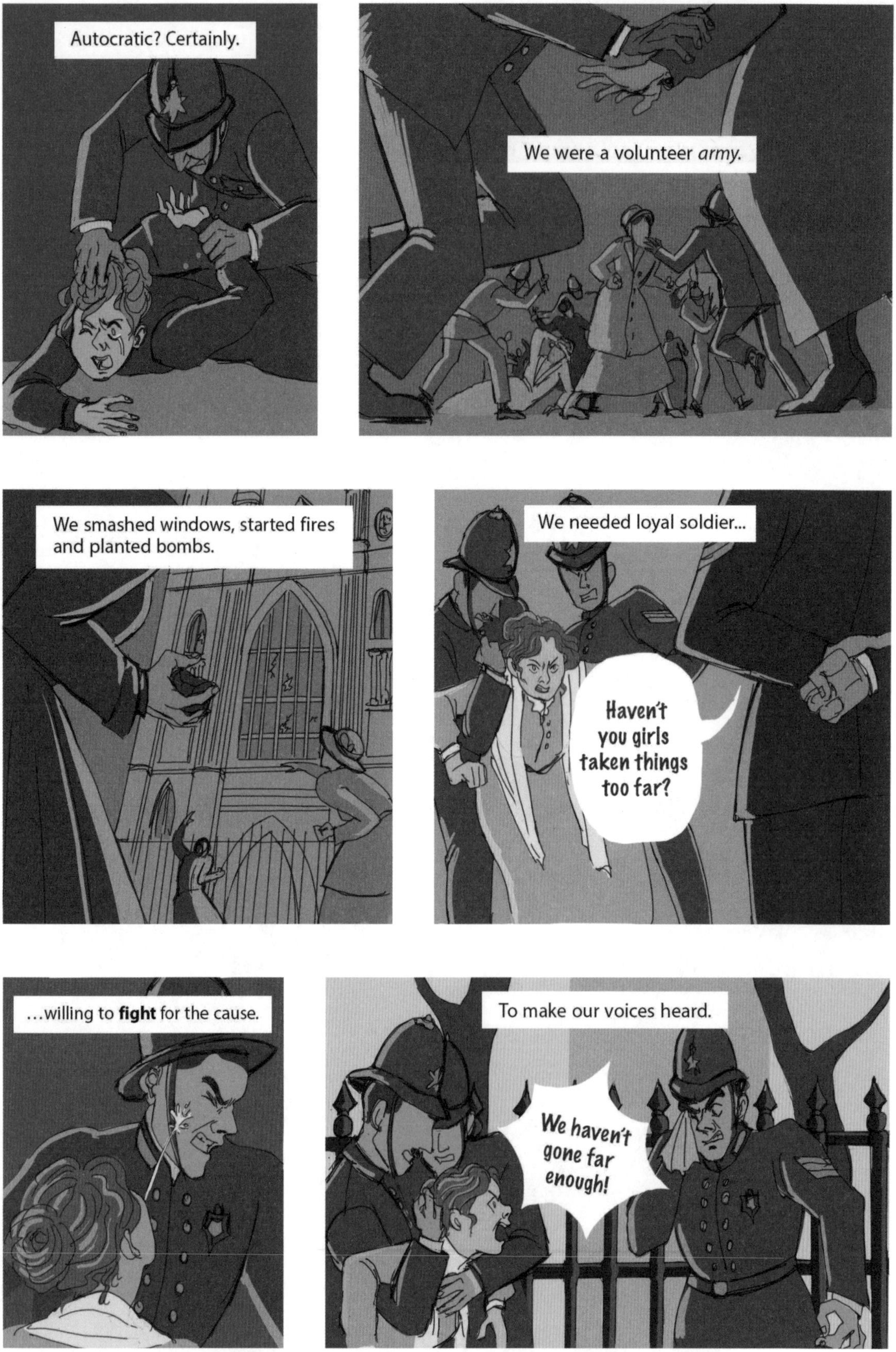
Autocratic? Certainly.
We were a volunteer *army*.
We smashed windows, started fires and planted bombs.
We needed loyal soldier...
Haven't you girls taken things too far?
...willing to **fight** for the cause.
To make our voices heard.
We haven't gone far enough!

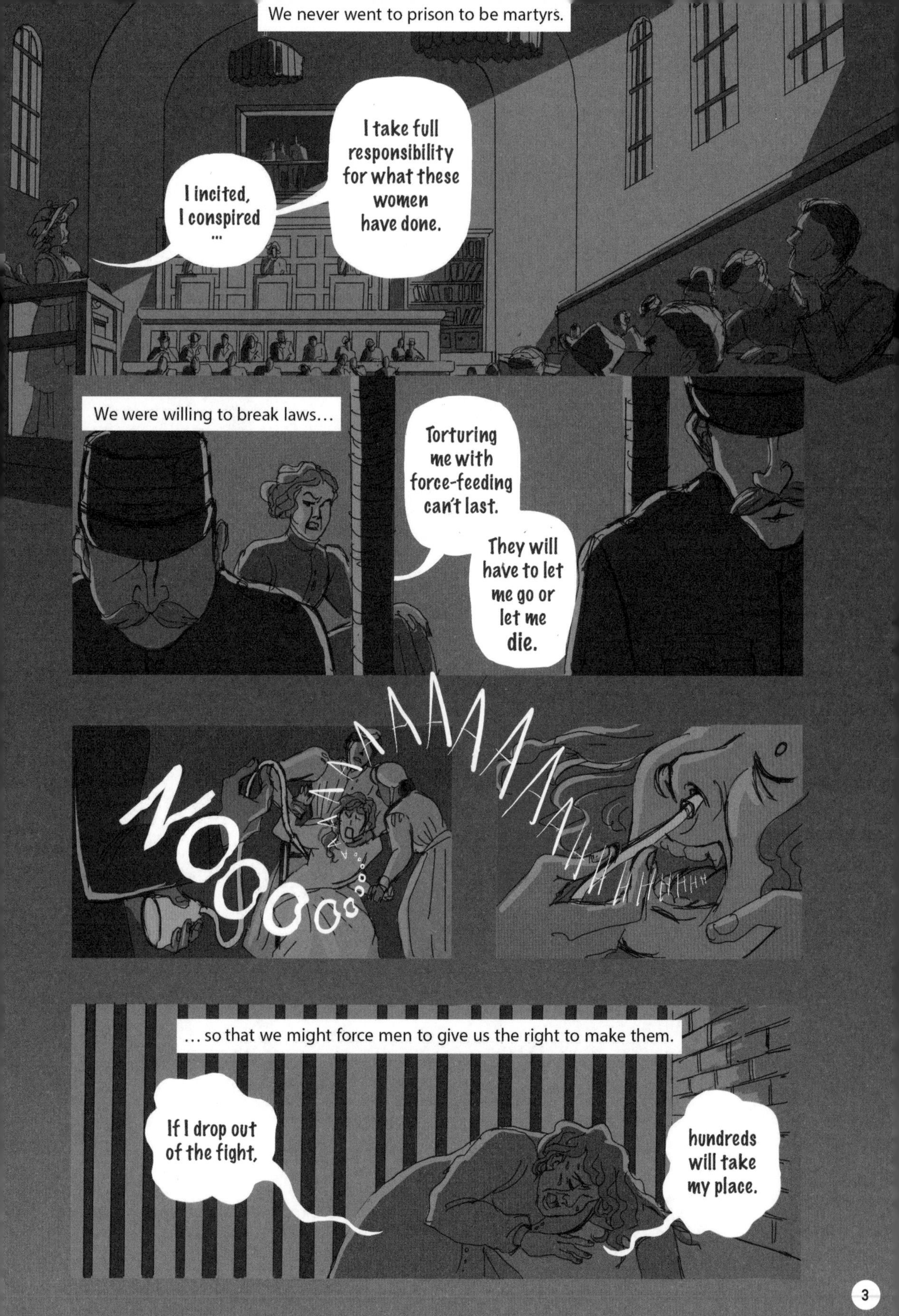
We never went to prison to be martyrs.
I incited, I conspired ...
I take full responsibility for what these women have done.
We were willing to break laws…
Torturing me with force-feeding can't last.
They will have to let me go or let me die.
… so that we might force men to give us the right to make them.
If I drop out of the fight,
hundreds will take my place.

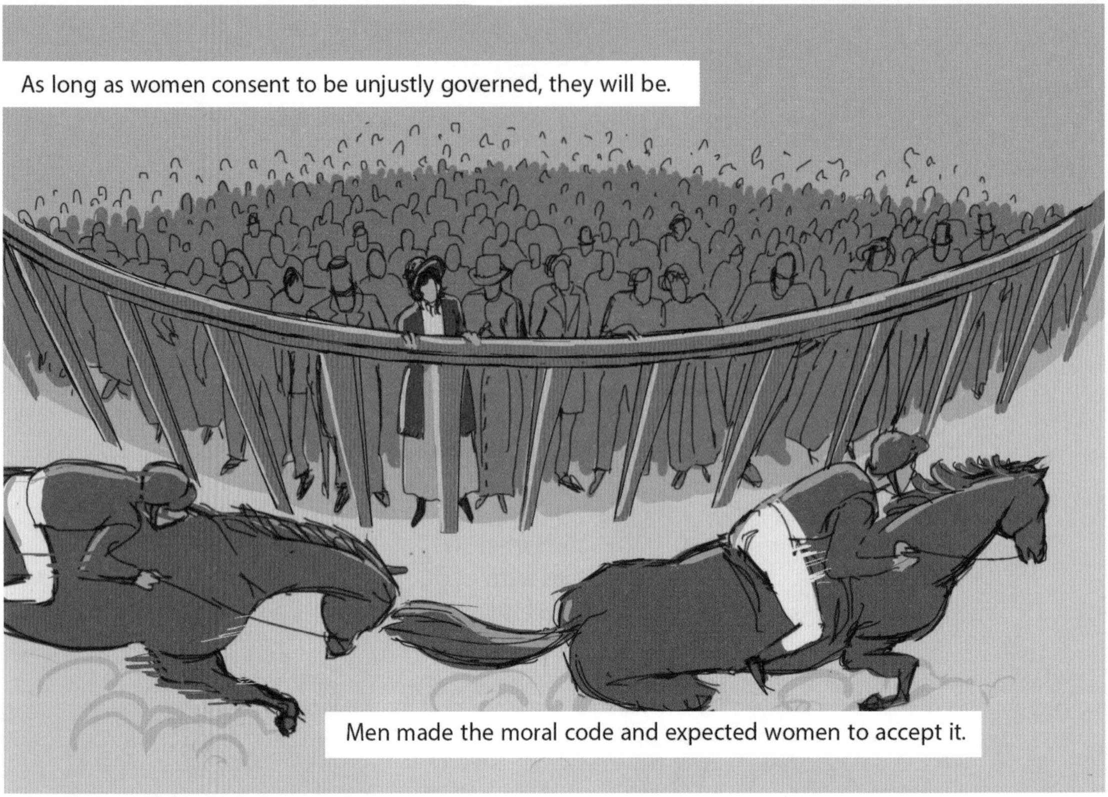

As long as women consent to be unjustly governed, they will be.
Men made the moral code and expected women to accept it.

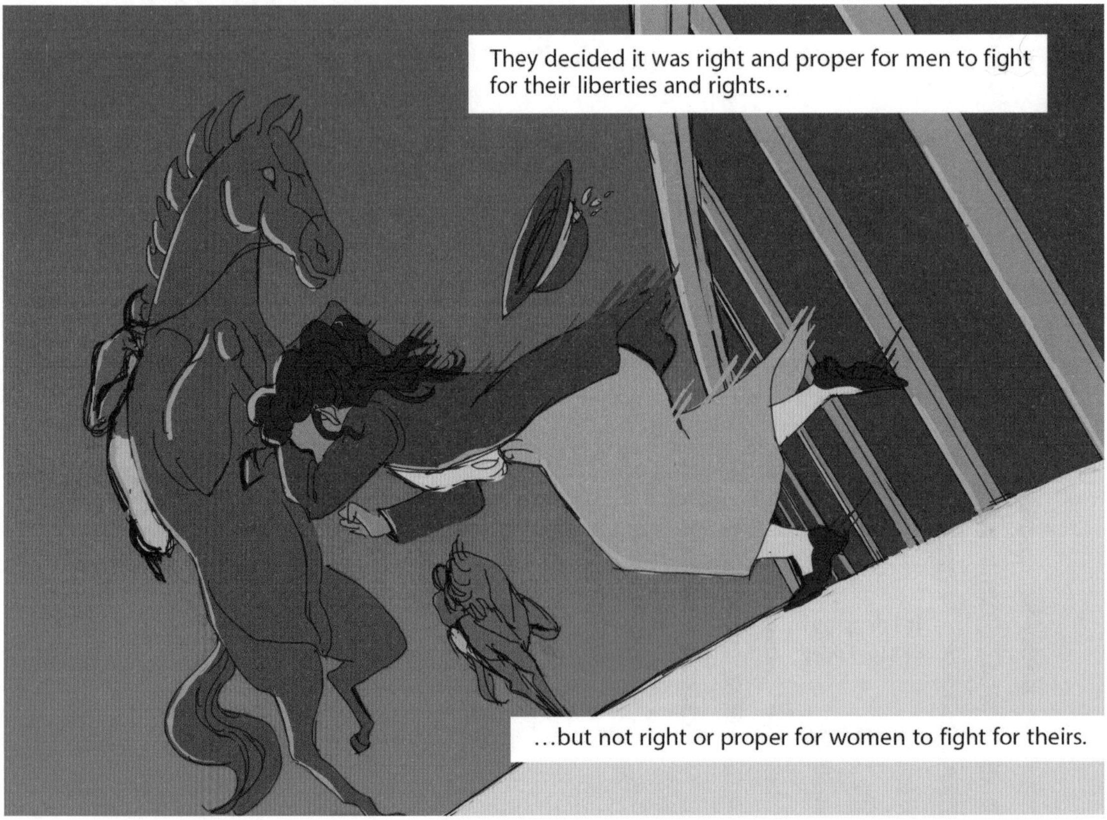

They decided it was right and proper for men to fight for their liberties and rights…
…but not right or proper for women to fight for theirs.

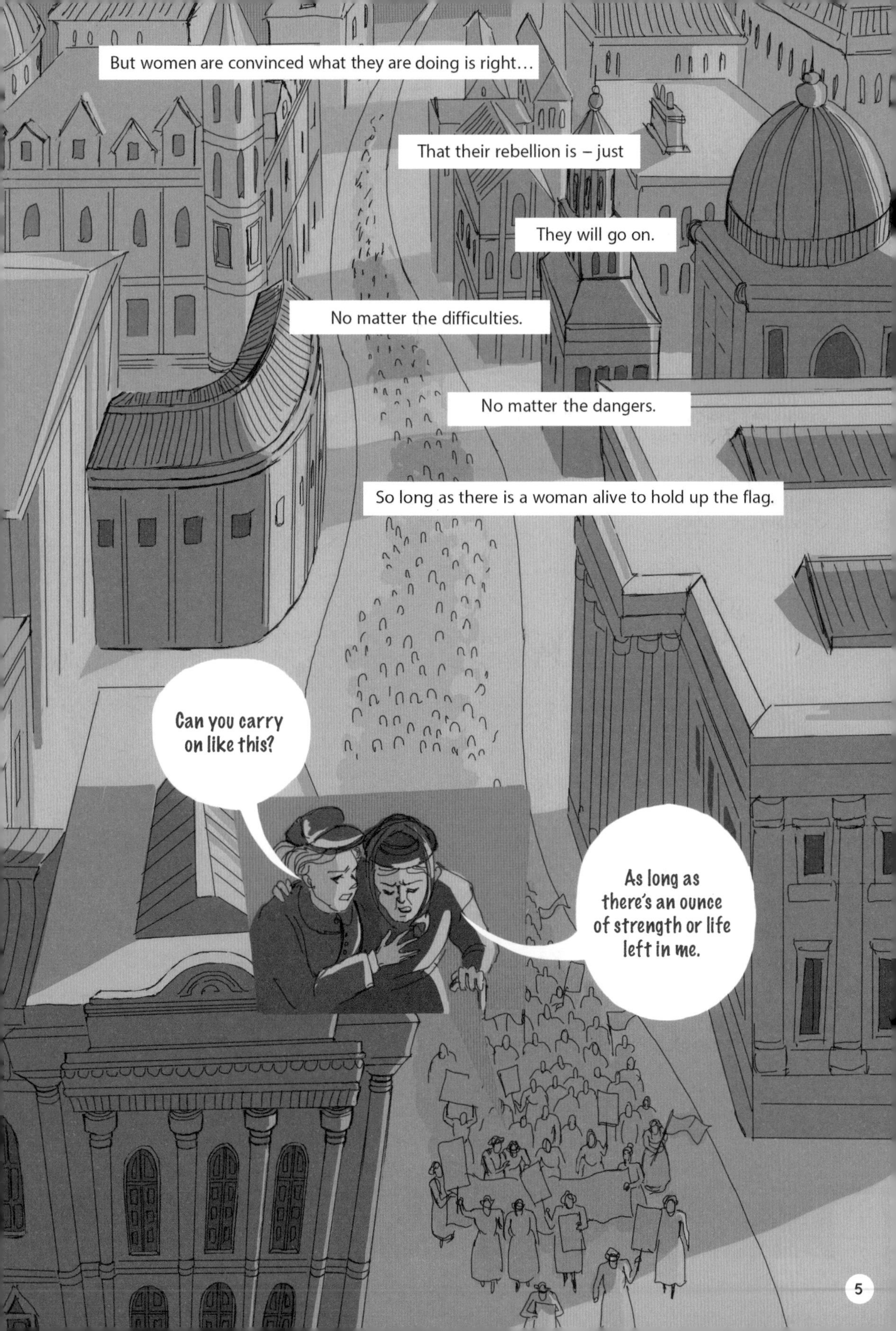

But women are convinced what they are doing is right…
That their rebellion is – just
They will go on.
No matter the difficulties.
No matter the dangers.
So long as there is a woman alive to hold up the flag.
Can you carry on like this?
As long as there's an ounce of strength or life left in me.

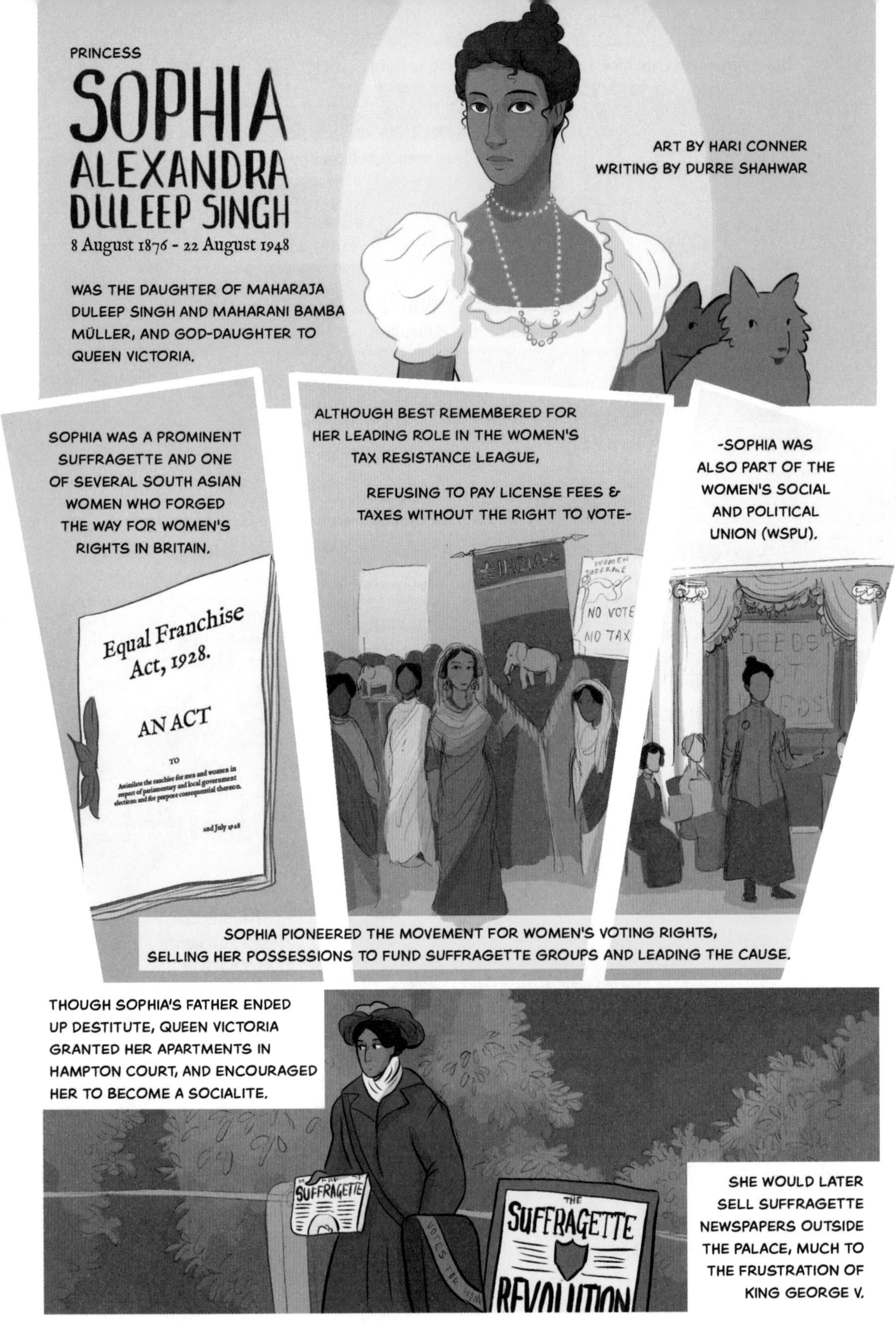

PRINCESS
SOPHIA ALEXANDRA DULEEP SINGH
8 August 1876 - 22 August 1948
ART BY HARI CONNER
WRITING BY DURRE SHAHWAR
WAS THE DAUGHTER OF MAHARAJA DULEEP SINGH AND MAHARANI BAMBA MÜLLER, AND GOD-DAUGHTER TO QUEEN VICTORIA.
SOPHIA WAS A PROMINENT SUFFRAGETTE AND ONE OF SEVERAL SOUTH ASIAN WOMEN WHO FORGED THE WAY FOR WOMEN'S RIGHTS IN BRITAIN.
Equal Franchise Act, 1928.
AN ACT
TO
ALTHOUGH BEST REMEMBERED FOR HER LEADING ROLE IN THE WOMEN'S TAX RESISTANCE LEAGUE,
REFUSING TO PAY LICENSE FEES & TAXES WITHOUT THE RIGHT TO VOTE-
INDIA
NO VOTE NO TAX
-SOPHIA WAS ALSO PART OF THE WOMEN'S SOCIAL AND POLITICAL UNION (WSPU).
SOPHIA PIONEERED THE MOVEMENT FOR WOMEN'S VOTING RIGHTS, SELLING HER POSSESSIONS TO FUND SUFFRAGETTE GROUPS AND LEADING THE CAUSE.
THOUGH SOPHIA'S FATHER ENDED UP DESTITUTE, QUEEN VICTORIA GRANTED HER APARTMENTS IN HAMPTON COURT, AND ENCOURAGED HER TO BECOME A SOCIALITE.
SUFFRAGETTE
THE SUFFRAGETTE
REVOLUTION
SHE WOULD LATER SELL SUFFRAGETTE NEWSPAPERS OUTSIDE THE PALACE, MUCH TO THE FRUSTRATION OF KING GEORGE V.

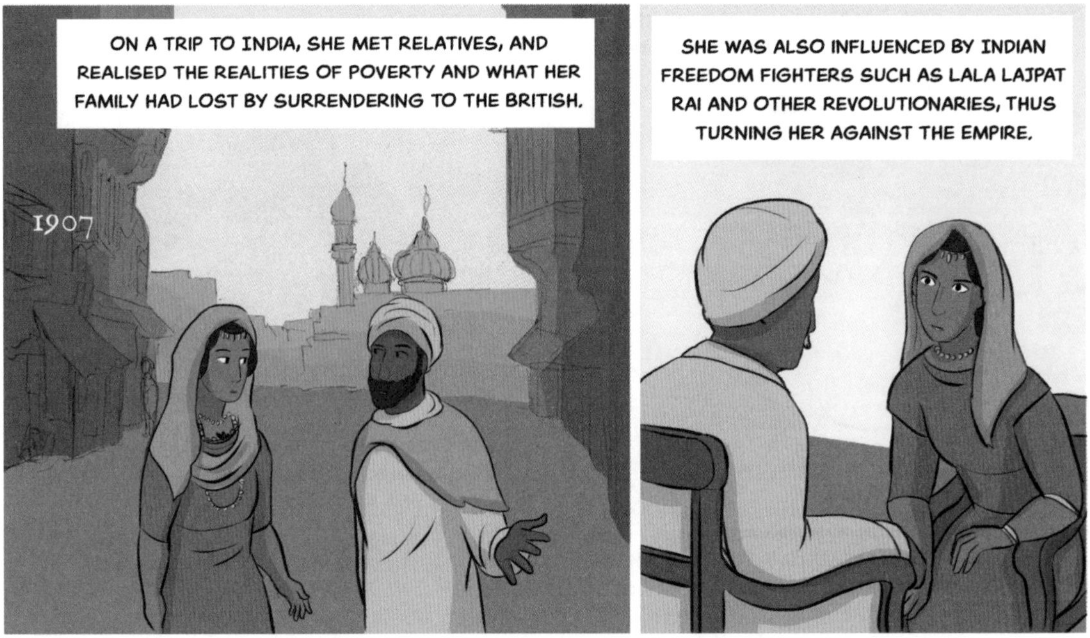
ON A TRIP TO INDIA, SHE MET RELATIVES, AND REALISED THE REALITIES OF POVERTY AND WHAT HER FAMILY HAD LOST BY SURRENDERING TO THE BRITISH.
1907
SHE WAS ALSO INFLUENCED BY INDIAN FREEDOM FIGHTERS SUCH AS LALA LAJPAT RAI AND OTHER REVOLUTIONARIES, THUS TURNING HER AGAINST THE EMPIRE.

SHE VALUED HER INDIAN HERITAGE, BUT WAS NOT BOUND BY ALLEGIANCE TO A SINGLE NATION AND SUPPORTED THE WOMEN'S CAUSE IN VARIOUS COUNTRIES.

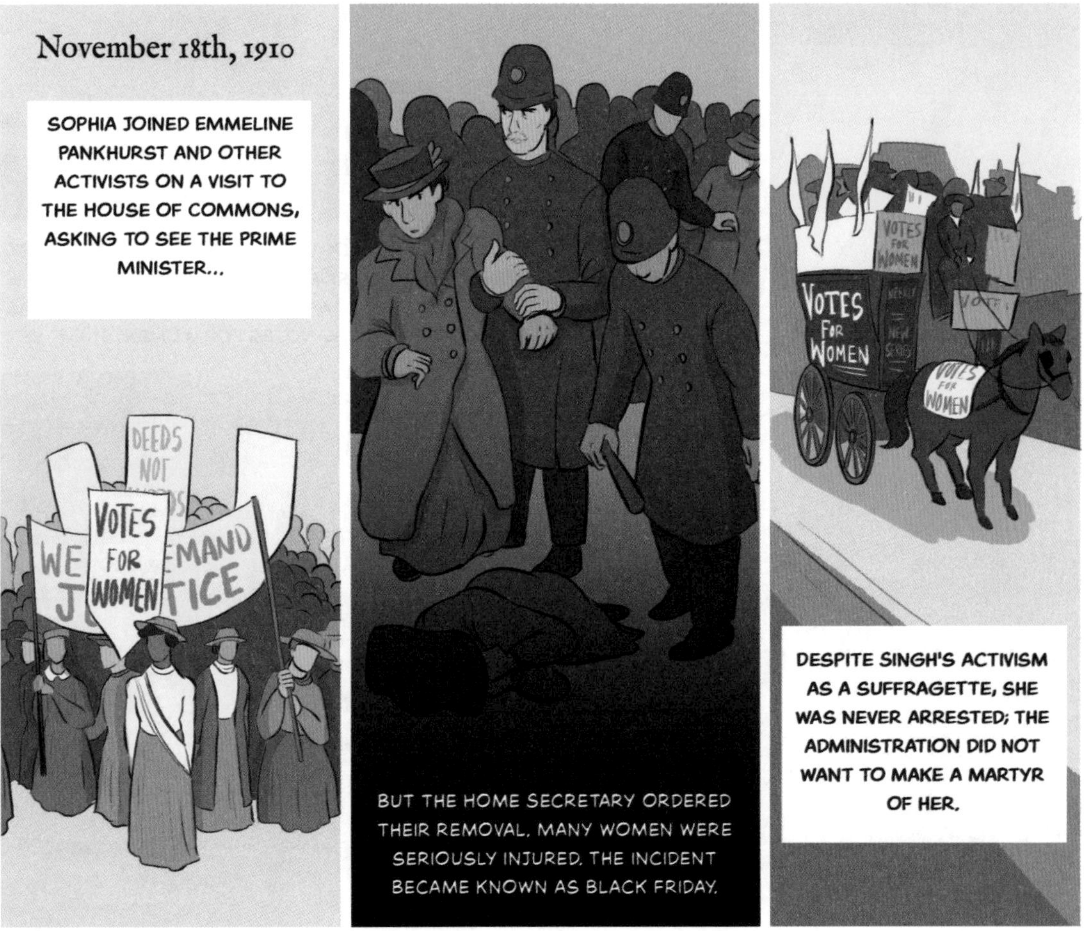
November 18th, 1910
SOPHIA JOINED EMMELINE PANKHURST AND OTHER ACTIVISTS ON A VISIT TO THE HOUSE OF COMMONS, ASKING TO SEE THE PRIME MINISTER...
DEEDS NOT
VOTES FOR WOMEN
WE EMAND
J TICE
BUT THE HOME SECRETARY ORDERED THEIR REMOVAL. MANY WOMEN WERE SERIOUSLY INJURED. THE INCIDENT BECAME KNOWN AS BLACK FRIDAY.
VOTES FOR WOMEN
VOTES FOR WOMEN
VOTES FOR WOMEN
DESPITE SINGH'S ACTIVISM AS A SUFFRAGETTE, SHE WAS NEVER ARRESTED; THE ADMINISTRATION DID NOT WANT TO MAKE A MARTYR OF HER.

DURING WW1, SINGH WAS A RED CROSS NURSE, TENDING TO WOUNDED INDIAN SOLDIERS WHO HAD BEEN EVACUATED FROM THE WESTERN FRONT.

SHE ORGANISED FLAG DAYS TO RAISE MONEY FOR WOUNDED SOLDIERS - REVOLUTIONARY AND SHOCKING AT THE TIME.

WHEN SHE MADE ANOTHER TRIP TO INDIA, SHE WAS MOBBED BY CROWDS WANTING TO SEE THE DAUGHTERS OF THE MAHARAJA. THIS BOOSTED FEMALE SUFFRAGE IN INDIA.

1924

£1.57

VOTES FOR WOMEN
Sophia Duleep Singh sells the Suffragett

SUFFRAGETTE

VOTES FOR WOMEN

AFTER THE DEATH OF FOUNDER EMMELINE PANKHURST, SOPHIA BECAME PRESIDENT OF THE COMMITTEE OF THE SUFFRAGETTE FELLOWSHIP, AND IN FEBRUARY 2018 WAS COMMEMORATED ON THE 'VOTES FOR WOMEN' STAMP SET.

SINGH DIED IN HER SLEEP ON 22 AUGUST 1948. SHE WISHED TO BE CREMATED ACCORDING TO SIKH RITES AND HER ASHES SPREAD IN INDIA.

SHE HAD DESCRIBED HER SOLE INTEREST AND LIFE'S PURPOSE AS "THE ADVANCEMENT OF WOMEN".

A PURPOSE WHICH SHE ACHIEVED.

A SHOUT OUT TO A SUPERHERO: HELEN BAMBER

WRITTEN BY SIANA BANGURA, ART BY LETTY WILSON

NOT ALL HEROES WEAR CAPES. BUT SOME ARE PSYCHOTHERAPISTS AND HUMAN RIGHTS ACTIVISTS – LIKE HELEN RAE BAMBER. BORN IN 1925 AND RAISED IN AMHURST PARK – A JEWISH AREA OF NORTH-EAST LONDON – SHE WAS THE DAUGHTER OF LOUIS BALMUTH (AN ACCOUNTANT BY DAY AND PHILOSOPHER, WRITER AND MATHEMATICIAN BY NIGHT) AND MARIE BADER (A SINGER AND PIANIST OF POLISH DESCENT).

ALTHOUGH HER MOTHER HOPED SHE'D BECOME A CELEBRATED PERFORMER, HELEN INSTEAD TOOK A JOB AS SECRETARY TO A HARLEY STREET DOCTOR, RESPONDING TO AN ADVERT CALLING FOR VOLUNTEERS TO HELP SURVIVORS OF NAZI CONCENTRATION CAMPS.

AT THE AGE OF 20, SHE JOINED ONE OF THE FIRST REHABILITATION TEAMS TO ENTER BERGEN-BELSEN CONCENTRATION CAMP WITH THE JEWISH RELIEF UNIT TO HELP WITH THE PHYSICAL AND PSYCHOLOGICAL RECOVERY OF MANY OF THE CAMP'S 20,000 HOLOCAUST SURVIVORS.

IN 2002, SHE RELATED HER EXPERIENCE AT BELSEN TO THE BBC AND SAID:

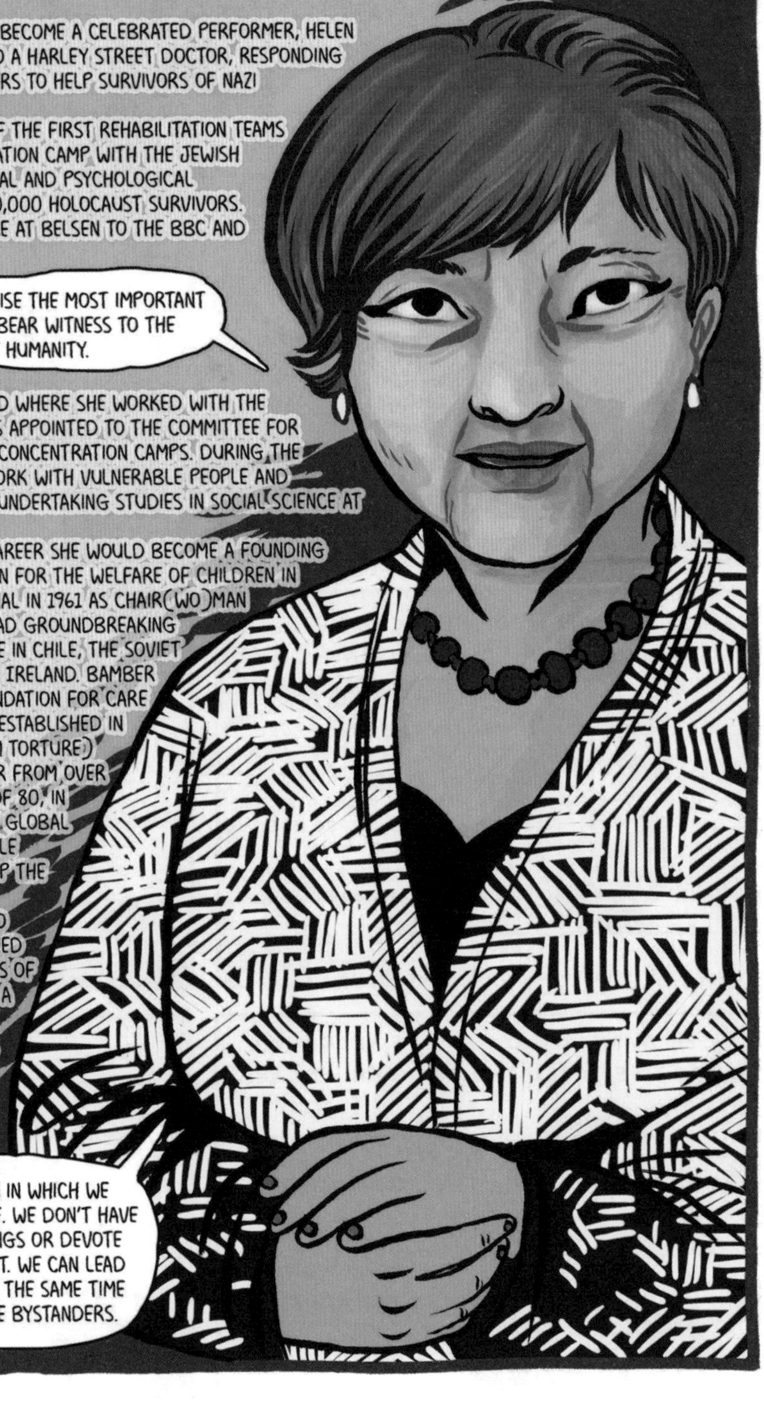
AFTER A WHILE I BEGAN TO REALISE THE MOST IMPORTANT ROLE FOR ME THERE WAS TO BEAR WITNESS TO THE VULNERABILITY OF HUMANITY.

IN 1947, HELEN RETURNED TO ENGLAND WHERE SHE WORKED WITH THE JEWISH REFUGEE COMMITTEE AND WAS APPOINTED TO THE COMMITTEE FOR THE CARE OF YOUNG CHILDREN FROM CONCENTRATION CAMPS. DURING THE NEXT EIGHT YEARS SHE TRAINED TO WORK WITH VULNERABLE PEOPLE AND SURVIVORS OF TRAUMA, WHILST ALSO UNDERTAKING STUDIES IN SOCIAL SCIENCE AT LSE.

OVER THE COURSE OF HER VIBRANT CAREER SHE WOULD BECOME A FOUNDING MEMBER OF THE NATIONAL ASSOCIATION FOR THE WELFARE OF CHILDREN IN HOSPITAL; JOIN AMNESTY INTERNATIONAL IN 1961 AS CHAIR(WO)MAN OF THE FIRST BRITISH GROUP; AND LEAD GROUNDBREAKING RESEARCH INTO GOVERNMENT TORTURE IN CHILE, THE SOVIET UNION, SOUTH AFRICA, AND NORTHERN IRELAND. BAMBER ALSO CO-FOUNDED THE MEDICAL FOUNDATION FOR CARE OF VICTIMS OF TORTURE. THE GROUP, ESTABLISHED IN 1985 (NOW KNOWN AS FREEDOM FROM TORTURE) TREATED UP TO 3,000 PATIENTS A YEAR FROM OVER 90 COUNTRIES.IN 2005, AT THE AGE OF 80, IN RESPONSE TO CHANGING PATTERNS OF GLOBAL VIOLENCE AND AN INCREASINGLY HOSTILE POLITICAL LANDSCAPE, BAMBER SET UP THE HELEN BAMBER FOUNDATION – THE CULMINATION OF HER LIFE'S WORK – TO EXPAND HER ALREADY WELL ESTABLISHED REHABILITATIVE WORK WITH SURVIVORS OF TORTURE.IN 2013, BAMBER RECEIVED A HUMAN RIGHTS AWARD FROM THE INSPIRATION AWARDS TO ADD TO HER LONG LIST OF HONOURS. IN AUGUST 2014, AT THE AGE OF 89, HELEN BAMBER DIED IN LONDON.

IN HER OWN WORDS:

THERE MAY BE WAYS IN WHICH WE CAN WORK FOR CHANGE. WE DON'T HAVE TO DO DRAMATIC THINGS OR DEVOTE OUR ENTIRE LIVES TO IT. WE CAN LEAD NORMAL LIVES BUT AT THE SAME TIME TRY HARD NOT TO BE BYSTANDERS.

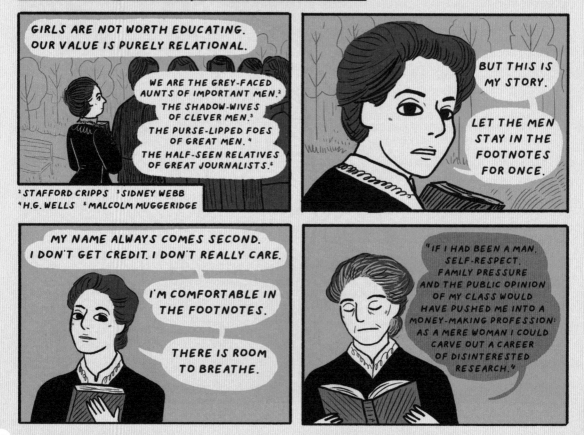

THE RADICAL IN THE FOOTNOTES

WRITTEN BY/ DENISE MINA   ILLUSTRATED BY/ MARIA STOIAN

GENESIS: EVE IS CREATED AS THE HELPMEET OF ADAM. IT IS THEREFORE RIGHT AND PROPER THAT, IN THE FOG OF HISTORY, WOMEN ARE ONLY EVER GLIMPSED.

READ THE BIOGRAPHIES OF THE GREAT MEN OF THE 20TH CENTURY. THERE I AM, IN THE FOOTNOTES.

ALWAYS IN THE FOOTNOTES.

HATEFUL, HEATHEN & DISGUSTING [1]

SECOND-TO-LAST OF NINE DAUGHTERS, BEATRICE WEBB HAS NOTHING TO DO BUT GROW UP, MARRY, AND BECOME AN ADJUNCT TO HER HUSBAND AND CHILDREN.

[1] OUR BELOVED QUEEN VICTORIA ON WOMEN SEEKING EQUALITY WITH MEN.

GIRLS ARE NOT WORTH EDUCATING. OUR VALUE IS PURELY RELATIONAL.

WE ARE THE GREY-FACED AUNTS OF IMPORTANT MEN. [2] THE SHADOW-WIVES OF CLEVER MEN. [3] THE PURSE-LIPPED FOES OF GREAT MEN. [4] THE HALF-SEEN RELATIVES OF GREAT JOURNALISTS. [5]

[2] STAFFORD CRIPPS [3] SIDNEY WEBB
[4] H.G. WELLS [5] MALCOLM MUGGERIDGE

BUT THIS IS MY STORY.

LET THE MEN STAY IN THE FOOTNOTES FOR ONCE.

MY NAME ALWAYS COMES SECOND. I DON'T GET CREDIT. I DON'T REALLY CARE.

I'M COMFORTABLE IN THE FOOTNOTES.

THERE IS ROOM TO BREATHE.

"IF I HAD BEEN A MAN, SELF-RESPECT, FAMILY PRESSURE AND THE PUBLIC OPINION OF MY CLASS WOULD HAVE PUSHED ME INTO A MONEY-MAKING PROFESSION: AS A MERE WOMAN I COULD CARVE OUT A CAREER OF DISINTERESTED RESEARCH." [6]

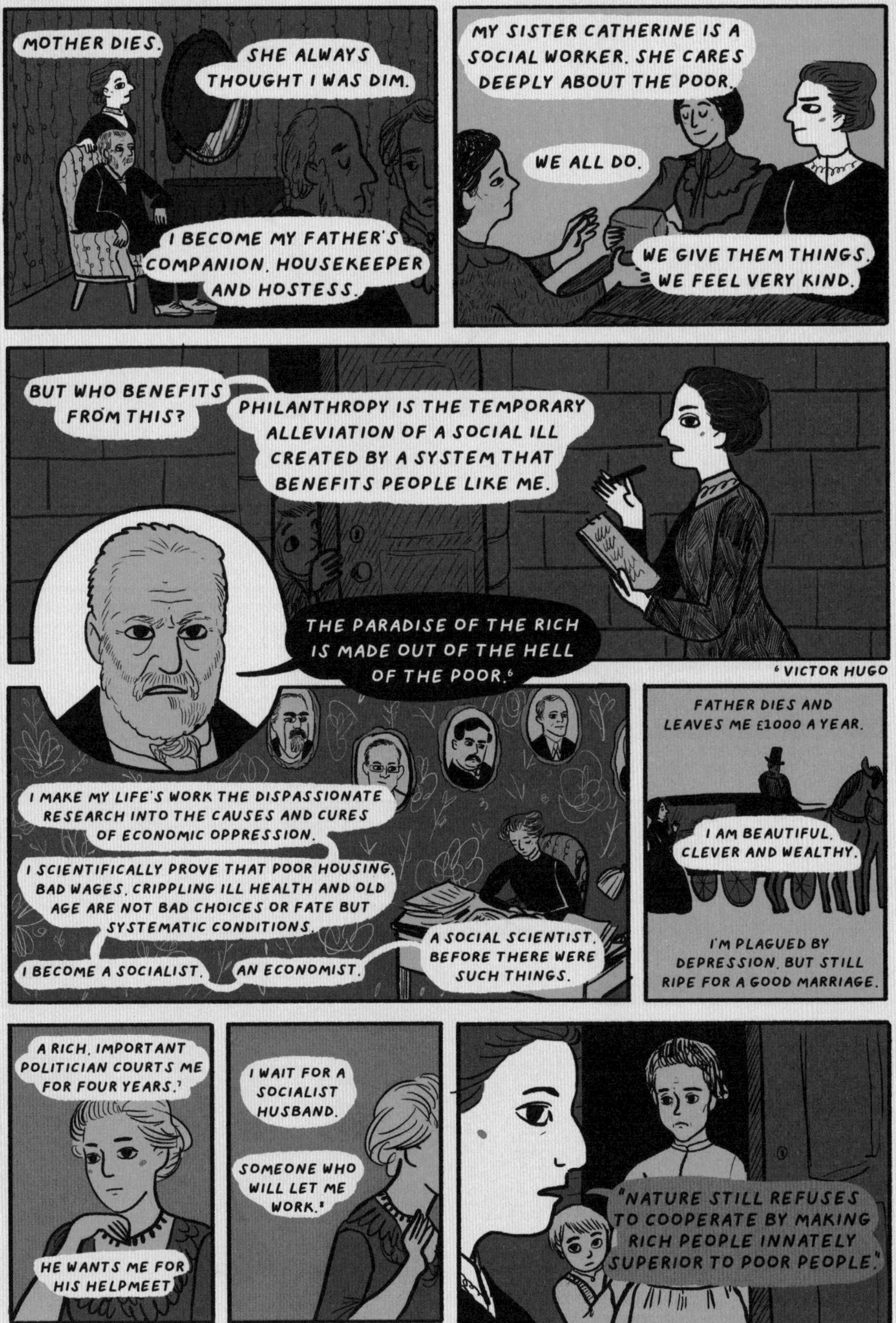
MOTHER DIES.
SHE ALWAYS THOUGHT I WAS DIM.
I BECOME MY FATHER'S COMPANION, HOUSEKEEPER AND HOSTESS.
MY SISTER CATHERINE IS A SOCIAL WORKER. SHE CARES DEEPLY ABOUT THE POOR.
WE ALL DO.
WE GIVE THEM THINGS. WE FEEL VERY KIND.
BUT WHO BENEFITS FROM THIS?
PHILANTHROPY IS THE TEMPORARY ALLEVIATION OF A SOCIAL ILL CREATED BY A SYSTEM THAT BENEFITS PEOPLE LIKE ME.
THE PARADISE OF THE RICH IS MADE OUT OF THE HELL OF THE POOR.[6]
I MAKE MY LIFE'S WORK THE DISPASSIONATE RESEARCH INTO THE CAUSES AND CURES OF ECONOMIC OPPRESSION.
I SCIENTIFICALLY PROVE THAT POOR HOUSING, BAD WAGES, CRIPPLING ILL HEALTH AND OLD AGE ARE NOT BAD CHOICES OR FATE BUT SYSTEMATIC CONDITIONS.
I BECOME A SOCIALIST.
AN ECONOMIST.
A SOCIAL SCIENTIST, BEFORE THERE WERE SUCH THINGS.
FATHER DIES AND LEAVES ME £1000 A YEAR.
I AM BEAUTIFUL, CLEVER AND WEALTHY.
I'M PLAGUED BY DEPRESSION, BUT STILL RIPE FOR A GOOD MARRIAGE.
A RICH, IMPORTANT POLITICIAN COURTS ME FOR FOUR YEARS.[7]
HE WANTS ME FOR HIS HELPMEET.
I WAIT FOR A SOCIALIST HUSBAND.
SOMEONE WHO WILL LET ME WORK.[8]
"NATURE STILL REFUSES TO COOPERATE BY MAKING RICH PEOPLE INNATELY SUPERIOR TO POOR PEOPLE."

[6] VICTOR HUGO

[7] JOSEPH CHAMBERLAIN

[8] SYDNEY WEBB

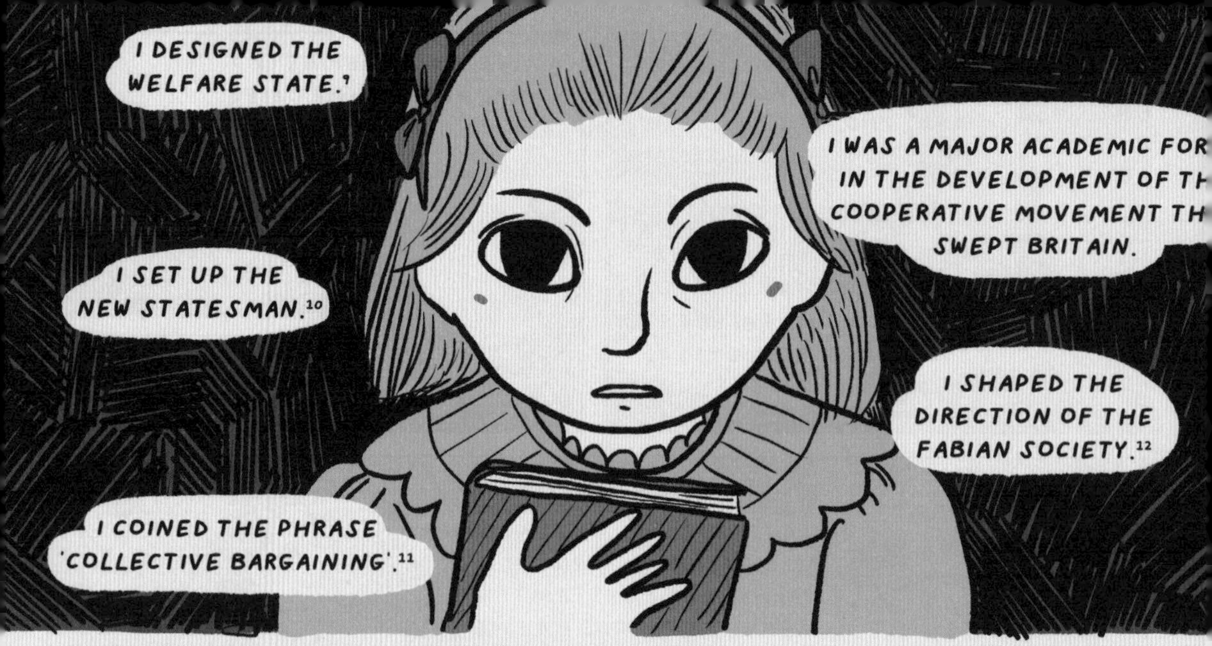
I DESIGNED THE WELFARE STATE.[9]
I WAS A MAJOR ACADEMIC FOR IN THE DEVELOPMENT OF TH COOPERATIVE MOVEMENT TH SWEPT BRITAIN.
I SET UP THE NEW STATESMAN.[10]
I SHAPED THE DIRECTION OF THE FABIAN SOCIETY.[12]
I COINED THE PHRASE 'COLLECTIVE BARGAINING'.[11]

[9] WILLIAM BEVERIDGE GOT THE CREDIT / [10] A WEEKLY MAGAZINE THAT SHAPED LEFTIST THINKING SINCE 1913
[11] REFERRING TO THE POWER OF WORKERS TO DEMAND BETTER WAGES AND CONDITIONS WHEN NEGOTIATING IN CONCERT / [12] A SOCIALIST THINK TANK, INSTRUMENTAL IN THE FORMATION OF THE LABOUR PARTY AND THE LONDON SCHOOL OF ECONOMICS.

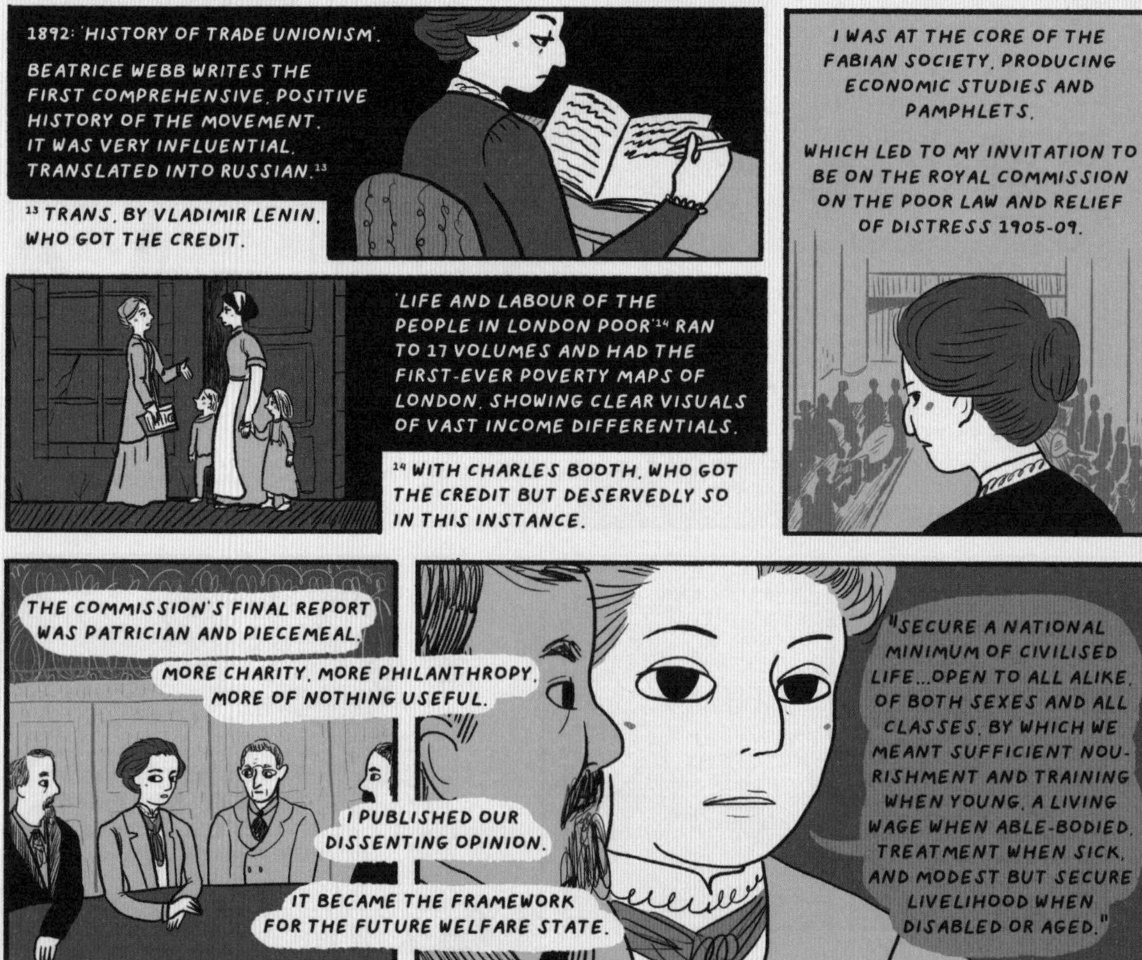
1892: 'HISTORY OF TRADE UNIONISM'.
BEATRICE WEBB WRITES THE FIRST COMPREHENSIVE, POSITIVE HISTORY OF THE MOVEMENT. IT WAS VERY INFLUENTIAL, TRANSLATED INTO RUSSIAN.[13]
[13] TRANS. BY VLADIMIR LENIN, WHO GOT THE CREDIT.
I WAS AT THE CORE OF THE FABIAN SOCIETY, PRODUCING ECONOMIC STUDIES AND PAMPHLETS.
WHICH LED TO MY INVITATION TO BE ON THE ROYAL COMMISSION ON THE POOR LAW AND RELIEF OF DISTRESS 1905-09.
'LIFE AND LABOUR OF THE PEOPLE IN LONDON POOR'[14] RAN TO 17 VOLUMES AND HAD THE FIRST-EVER POVERTY MAPS OF LONDON, SHOWING CLEAR VISUALS OF VAST INCOME DIFFERENTIALS.
[14] WITH CHARLES BOOTH, WHO GOT THE CREDIT BUT DESERVEDLY SO IN THIS INSTANCE.
THE COMMISSION'S FINAL REPORT WAS PATRICIAN AND PIECEMEAL.
MORE CHARITY, MORE PHILANTHROPY, MORE OF NOTHING USEFUL.
I PUBLISHED OUR DISSENTING OPINION.
IT BECAME THE FRAMEWORK FOR THE FUTURE WELFARE STATE.
"SECURE A NATIONAL MINIMUM OF CIVILISED LIFE...OPEN TO ALL ALIKE, OF BOTH SEXES AND ALL CLASSES, BY WHICH WE MEANT SUFFICIENT NOURISHMENT AND TRAINING WHEN YOUNG, A LIVING WAGE WHEN ABLE-BODIED, TREATMENT WHEN SICK, AND MODEST BUT SECURE LIVELIHOOD WHEN DISABLED OR AGED."

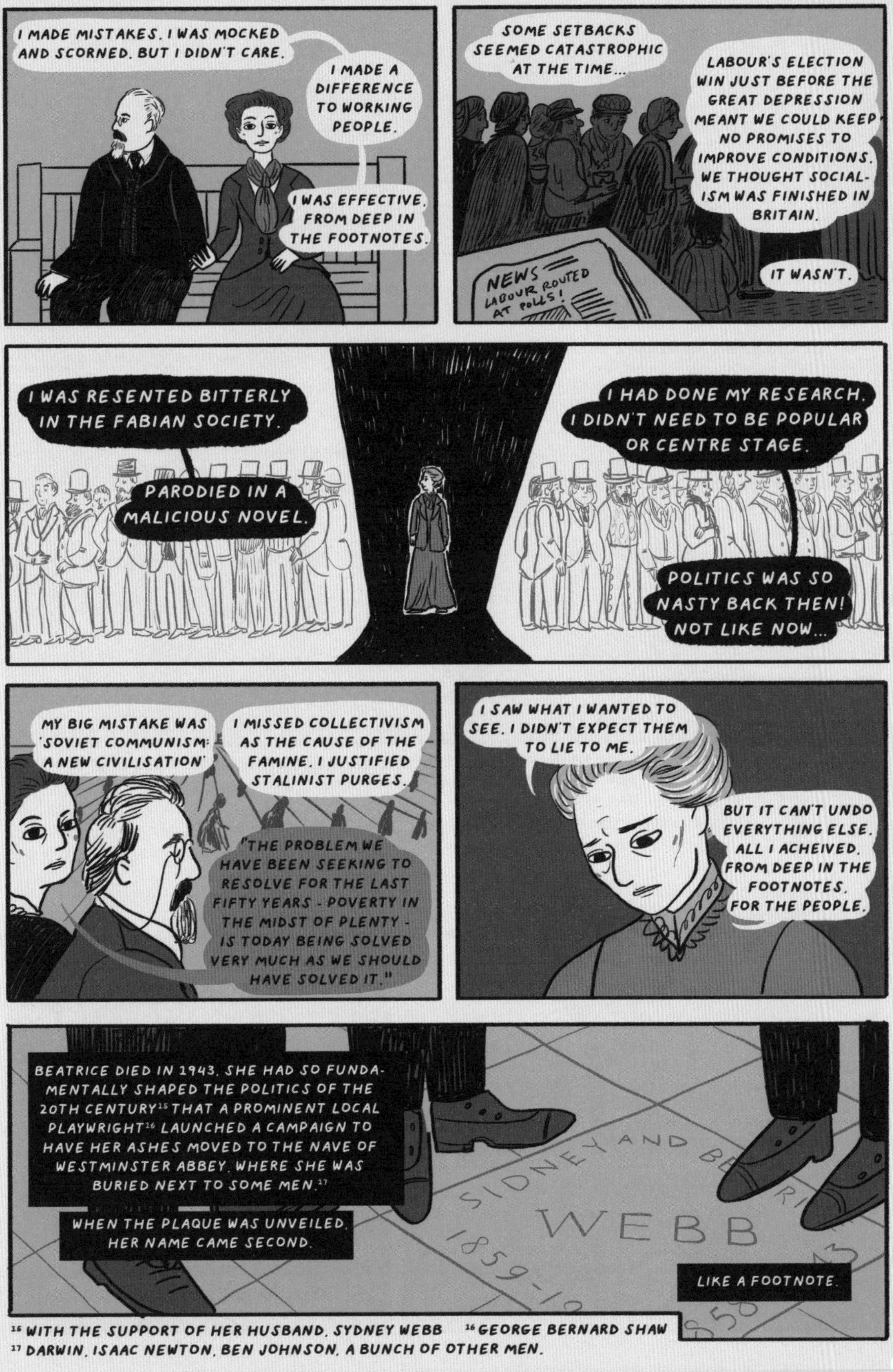

I MADE MISTAKES. I WAS MOCKED AND SCORNED. BUT I DIDN'T CARE.
I MADE A DIFFERENCE TO WORKING PEOPLE.
I WAS EFFECTIVE. FROM DEEP IN THE FOOTNOTES.
SOME SETBACKS SEEMED CATASTROPHIC AT THE TIME...
LABOUR'S ELECTION WIN JUST BEFORE THE GREAT DEPRESSION MEANT WE COULD KEEP NO PROMISES TO IMPROVE CONDITIONS. WE THOUGHT SOCIALISM WAS FINISHED IN BRITAIN.
IT WASN'T.
NEWS
LABOUR ROUTED AT POLLS!
I WAS RESENTED BITTERLY IN THE FABIAN SOCIETY.
PARODIED IN A MALICIOUS NOVEL.
I HAD DONE MY RESEARCH. I DIDN'T NEED TO BE POPULAR OR CENTRE STAGE.
POLITICS WAS SO NASTY BACK THEN! NOT LIKE NOW...
MY BIG MISTAKE WAS 'SOVIET COMMUNISM: A NEW CIVILISATION'
I MISSED COLLECTIVISM AS THE CAUSE OF THE FAMINE. I JUSTIFIED STALINIST PURGES.
"THE PROBLEM WE HAVE BEEN SEEKING TO RESOLVE FOR THE LAST FIFTY YEARS - POVERTY IN THE MIDST OF PLENTY - IS TODAY BEING SOLVED VERY MUCH AS WE SHOULD HAVE SOLVED IT."
I SAW WHAT I WANTED TO SEE. I DIDN'T EXPECT THEM TO LIE TO ME.
BUT IT CAN'T UNDO EVERYTHING ELSE. ALL I ACHEIVED. FROM DEEP IN THE FOOTNOTES. FOR THE PEOPLE.
BEATRICE DIED IN 1943. SHE HAD SO FUNDAMENTALLY SHAPED THE POLITICS OF THE 20TH CENTURY[15] THAT A PROMINENT LOCAL PLAYWRIGHT[16] LAUNCHED A CAMPAIGN TO HAVE HER ASHES MOVED TO THE NAVE OF WESTMINSTER ABBEY. WHERE SHE WAS BURIED NEXT TO SOME MEN.[17]
WHEN THE PLAQUE WAS UNVEILED. HER NAME CAME SECOND.
SIDNEY AND BE
WEBB
1859-1
LIKE A FOOTNOTE.

[15] WITH THE SUPPORT OF HER HUSBAND. SYDNEY WEBB [16] GEORGE BERNARD SHAW
[17] DARWIN. ISAAC NEWTON. BEN JOHNSON. A BUNCH OF OTHER MEN.

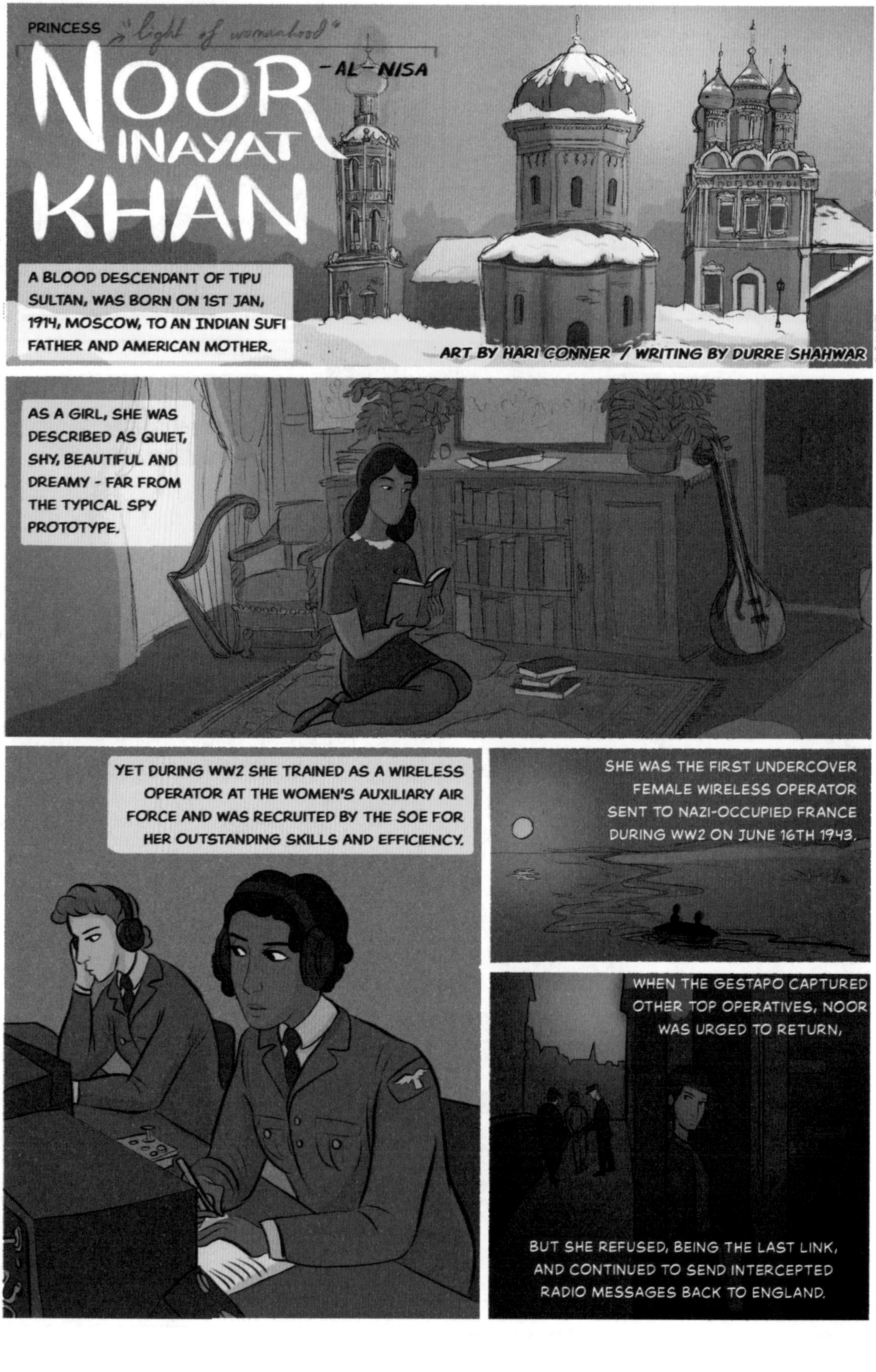
PRINCESS
"light of womanhood"
NOOR -AL-NISA
INAYAT
KHAN
A BLOOD DESCENDANT OF TIPU SULTAN, WAS BORN ON 1ST JAN, 1914, MOSCOW, TO AN INDIAN SUFI FATHER AND AMERICAN MOTHER.
ART BY HARI CONNER / WRITING BY DURRE SHAHWAR
AS A GIRL, SHE WAS DESCRIBED AS QUIET, SHY, BEAUTIFUL AND DREAMY - FAR FROM THE TYPICAL SPY PROTOTYPE.
YET DURING WW2 SHE TRAINED AS A WIRELESS OPERATOR AT THE WOMEN'S AUXILIARY AIR FORCE AND WAS RECRUITED BY THE SOE FOR HER OUTSTANDING SKILLS AND EFFICIENCY.
SHE WAS THE FIRST UNDERCOVER FEMALE WIRELESS OPERATOR SENT TO NAZI-OCCUPIED FRANCE DURING WW2 ON JUNE 16TH 1943.
WHEN THE GESTAPO CAPTURED OTHER TOP OPERATIVES, NOOR WAS URGED TO RETURN,
BUT SHE REFUSED, BEING THE LAST LINK, AND CONTINUED TO SEND INTERCEPTED RADIO MESSAGES BACK TO ENGLAND.

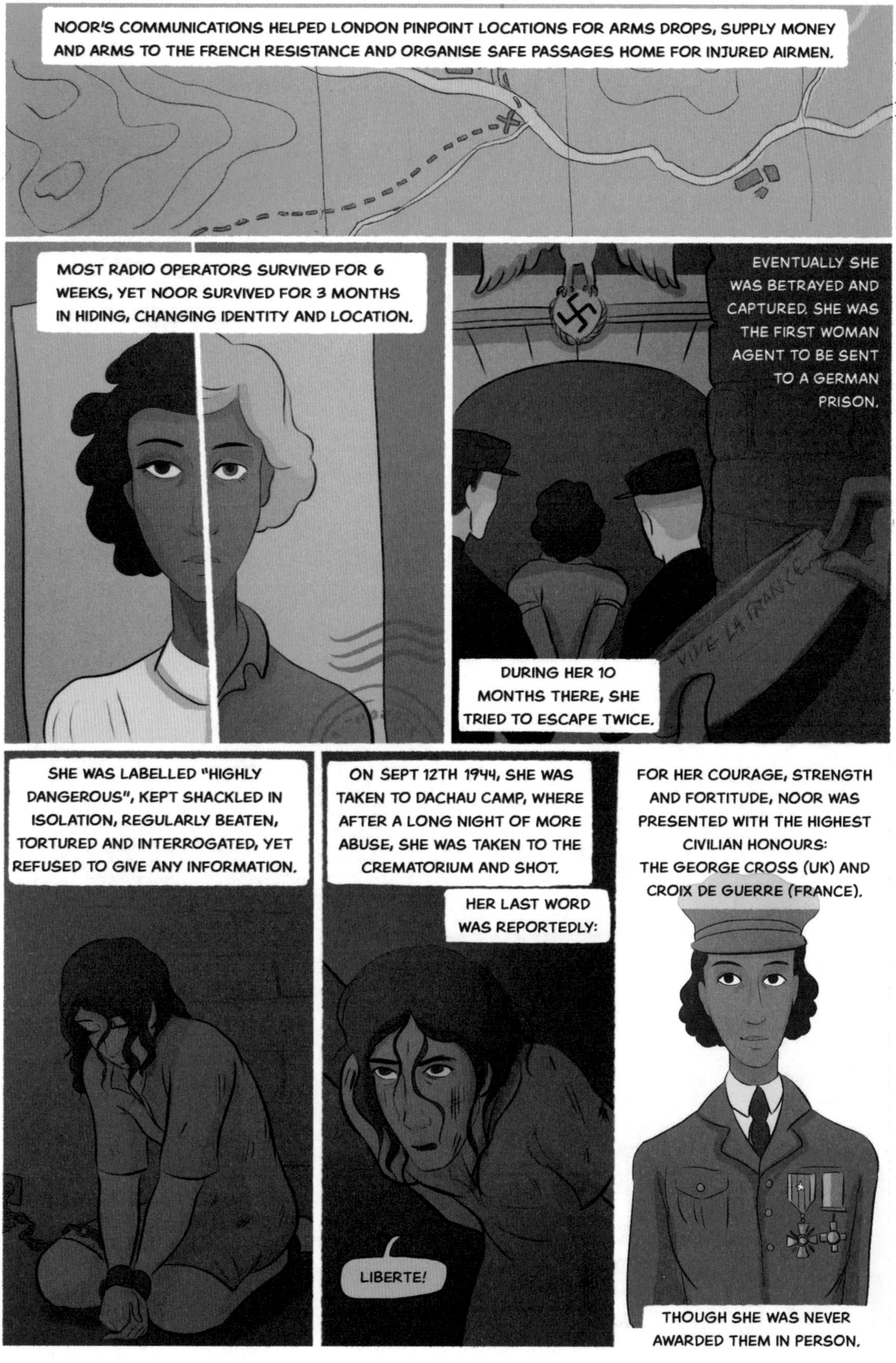
NOOR'S COMMUNICATIONS HELPED LONDON PINPOINT LOCATIONS FOR ARMS DROPS, SUPPLY MONEY AND ARMS TO THE FRENCH RESISTANCE AND ORGANISE SAFE PASSAGES HOME FOR INJURED AIRMEN.
MOST RADIO OPERATORS SURVIVED FOR 6 WEEKS, YET NOOR SURVIVED FOR 3 MONTHS IN HIDING, CHANGING IDENTITY AND LOCATION.
EVENTUALLY SHE WAS BETRAYED AND CAPTURED. SHE WAS THE FIRST WOMAN AGENT TO BE SENT TO A GERMAN PRISON.
VIVE LA FRANCE
DURING HER 10 MONTHS THERE, SHE TRIED TO ESCAPE TWICE.
SHE WAS LABELLED "HIGHLY DANGEROUS", KEPT SHACKLED IN ISOLATION, REGULARLY BEATEN, TORTURED AND INTERROGATED, YET REFUSED TO GIVE ANY INFORMATION.
ON SEPT 12TH 1944, SHE WAS TAKEN TO DACHAU CAMP, WHERE AFTER A LONG NIGHT OF MORE ABUSE, SHE WAS TAKEN TO THE CREMATORIUM AND SHOT.
HER LAST WORD WAS REPORTEDLY:
LIBERTE!
FOR HER COURAGE, STRENGTH AND FORTITUDE, NOOR WAS PRESENTED WITH THE HIGHEST CIVILIAN HONOURS: THE GEORGE CROSS (UK) AND CROIX DE GUERRE (FRANCE).
THOUGH SHE WAS NEVER AWARDED THEM IN PERSON.

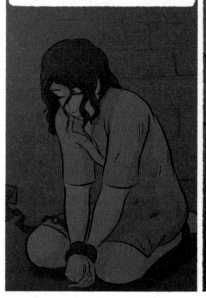

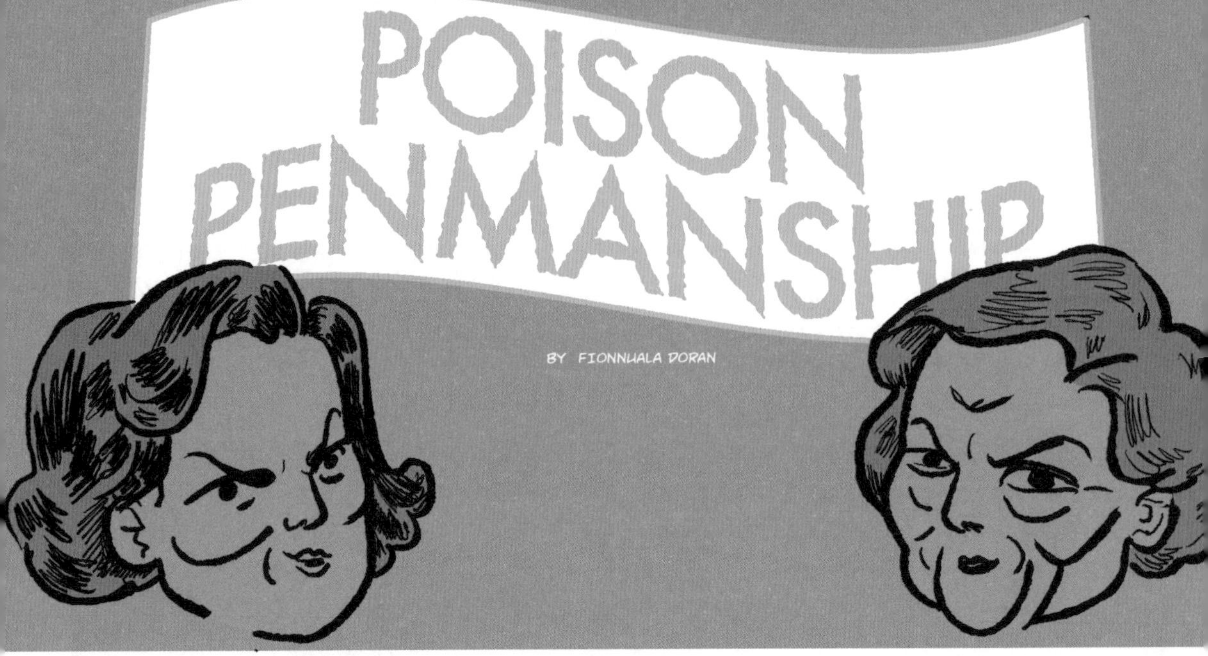
POISON PENMANSHIP
BY FIONNUALA DORAN

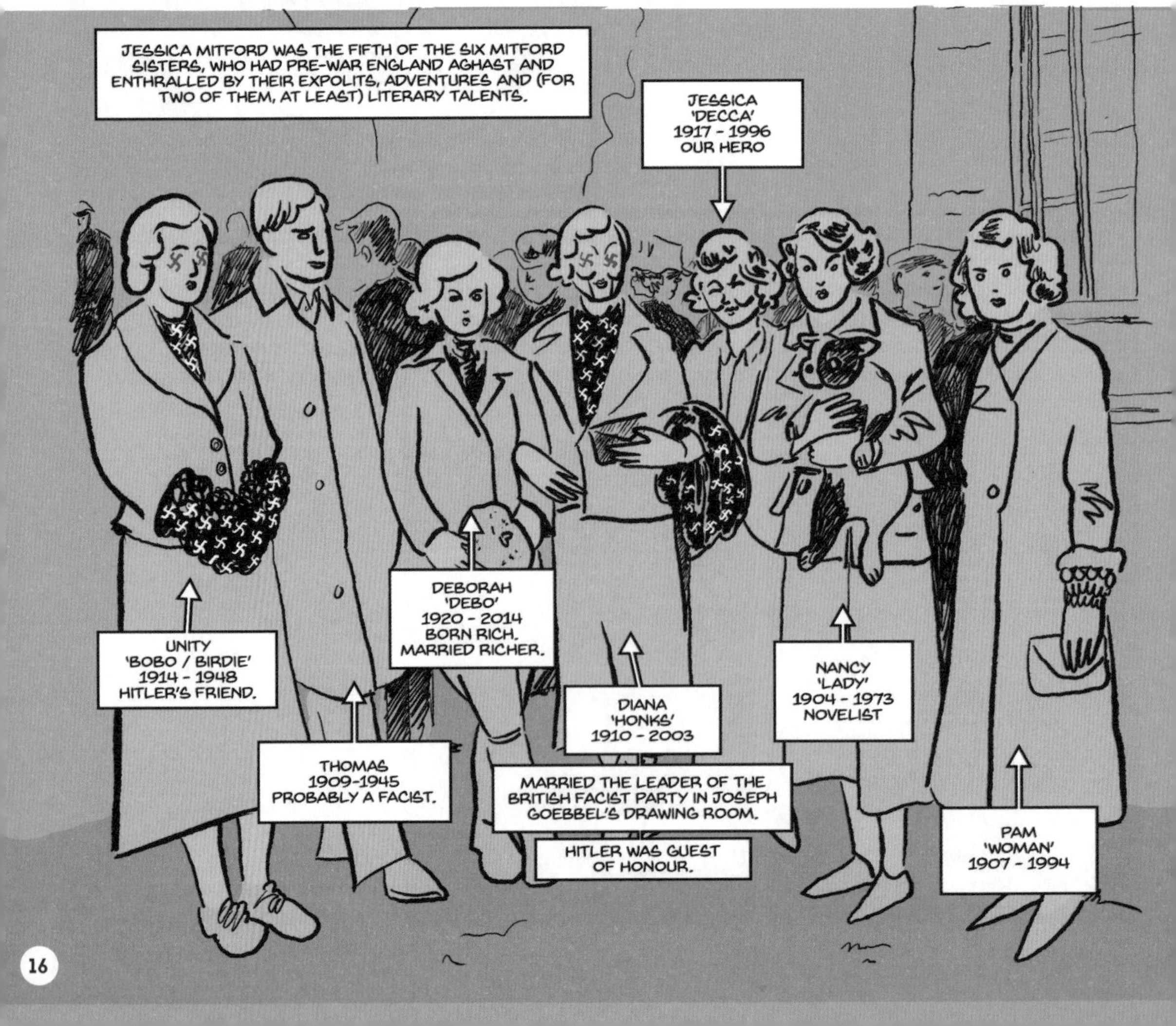
JESSICA MITFORD WAS THE FIFTH OF THE SIX MITFORD SISTERS, WHO HAD PRE-WAR ENGLAND AGHAST AND ENTHRALLED BY THEIR EXPOLITS, ADVENTURES AND (FOR TWO OF THEM, AT LEAST) LITERARY TALENTS.
JESSICA 'DECCA' 1917 - 1996 OUR HERO
UNITY 'BOBO / BIRDIE' 1914 - 1948 HITLER'S FRIEND.
THOMAS 1909-1945 PROBABLY A FACIST.
DEBORAH 'DEBO' 1920 - 2014 BORN RICH. MARRIED RICHER.
DIANA 'HONKS' 1910 - 2003
MARRIED THE LEADER OF THE BRITISH FACIST PARTY IN JOSEPH GOEBBEL'S DRAWING ROOM.
HITLER WAS GUEST OF HONOUR.
NANCY 'LADY' 1904 - 1973 NOVELIST
PAM 'WOMAN' 1907 - 1994

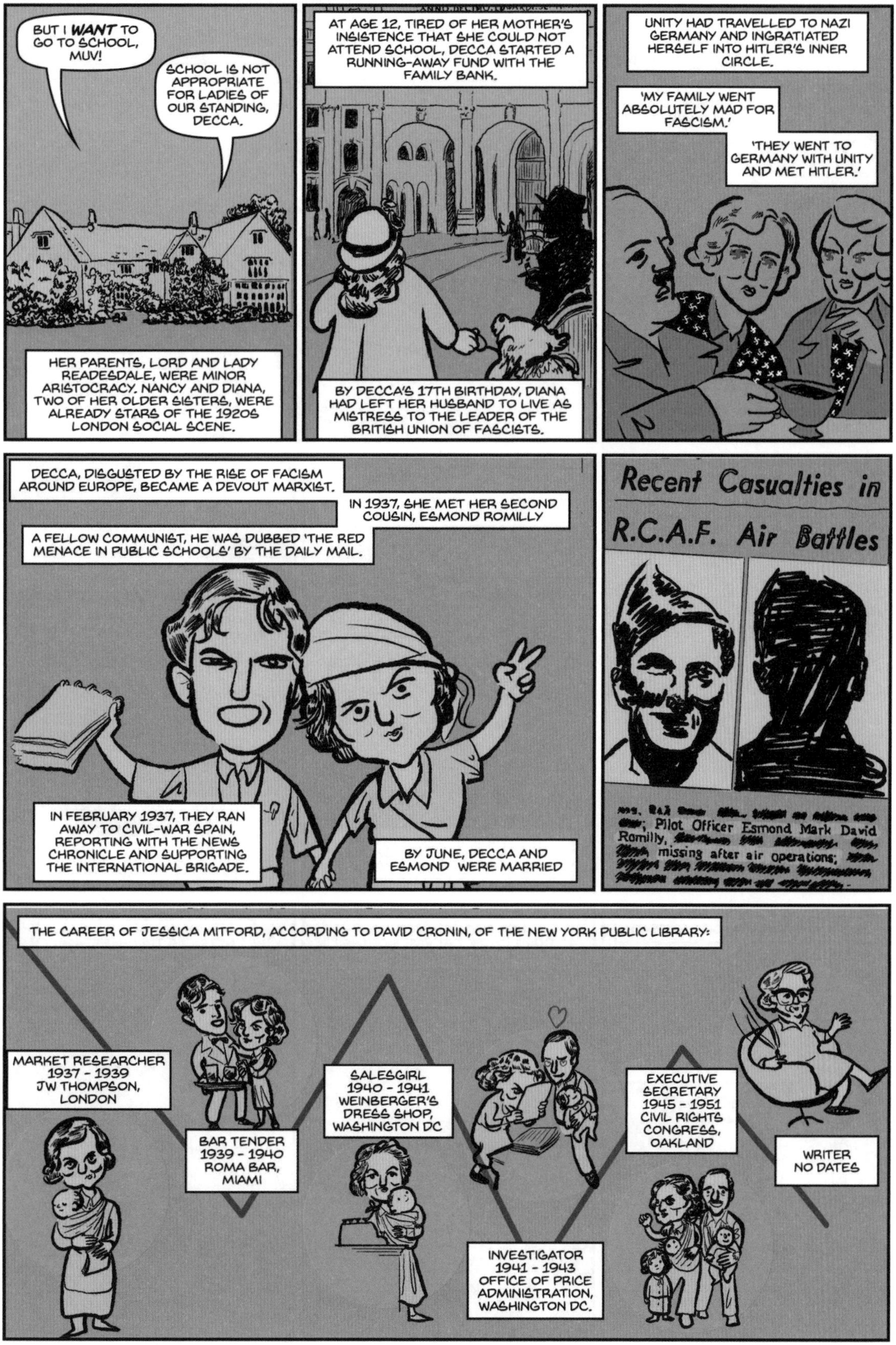
BUT I WANT TO GO TO SCHOOL, MUV!
SCHOOL IS NOT APPROPRIATE FOR LADIES OF OUR STANDING, DECCA.
HER PARENTS, LORD AND LADY READESDALE, WERE MINOR ARISTOCRACY. NANCY AND DIANA, TWO OF HER OLDER SISTERS, WERE ALREADY STARS OF THE 1920S LONDON SOCIAL SCENE.
AT AGE 12, TIRED OF HER MOTHER'S INSISTENCE THAT SHE COULD NOT ATTEND SCHOOL, DECCA STARTED A RUNNING-AWAY FUND WITH THE FAMILY BANK.
BY DECCA'S 17TH BIRTHDAY, DIANA HAD LEFT HER HUSBAND TO LIVE AS MISTRESS TO THE LEADER OF THE BRITISH UNION OF FASCISTS.
UNITY HAD TRAVELLED TO NAZI GERMANY AND INGRATIATED HERSELF INTO HITLER'S INNER CIRCLE.
'MY FAMILY WENT ABSOLUTELY MAD FOR FASCISM.'
'THEY WENT TO GERMANY WITH UNITY AND MET HITLER.'
DECCA, DISGUSTED BY THE RISE OF FACISM AROUND EUROPE, BECAME A DEVOUT MARXIST.
IN 1937, SHE MET HER SECOND COUSIN, ESMOND ROMILLY
A FELLOW COMMUNIST, HE WAS DUBBED 'THE RED MENACE IN PUBLIC SCHOOLS' BY THE DAILY MAIL.
IN FEBRUARY 1937, THEY RAN AWAY TO CIVIL-WAR SPAIN, REPORTING WITH THE NEWS CHRONICLE AND SUPPORTING THE INTERNATIONAL BRIGADE.
BY JUNE, DECCA AND ESMOND WERE MARRIED
Recent Casualties in R.C.A.F. Air Battles
[redacted]; Pilot Officer Esmond Mark David Romilly, [redacted] missing after air operations; [redacted]
THE CAREER OF JESSICA MITFORD, ACCORDING TO DAVID CRONIN, OF THE NEW YORK PUBLIC LIBRARY:
MARKET RESEARCHER 1937 - 1939 JW THOMPSON, LONDON
BAR TENDER 1939 - 1940 ROMA BAR, MIAMI
SALESGIRL 1940 - 1941 WEINBERGER'S DRESS SHOP, WASHINGTON DC
INVESTIGATOR 1941 - 1943 OFFICE OF PRICE ADMINISTRATION, WASHINGTON DC.
EXECUTIVE SECRETARY 1945 - 1951 CIVIL RIGHTS CONGRESS, OAKLAND
WRITER NO DATES

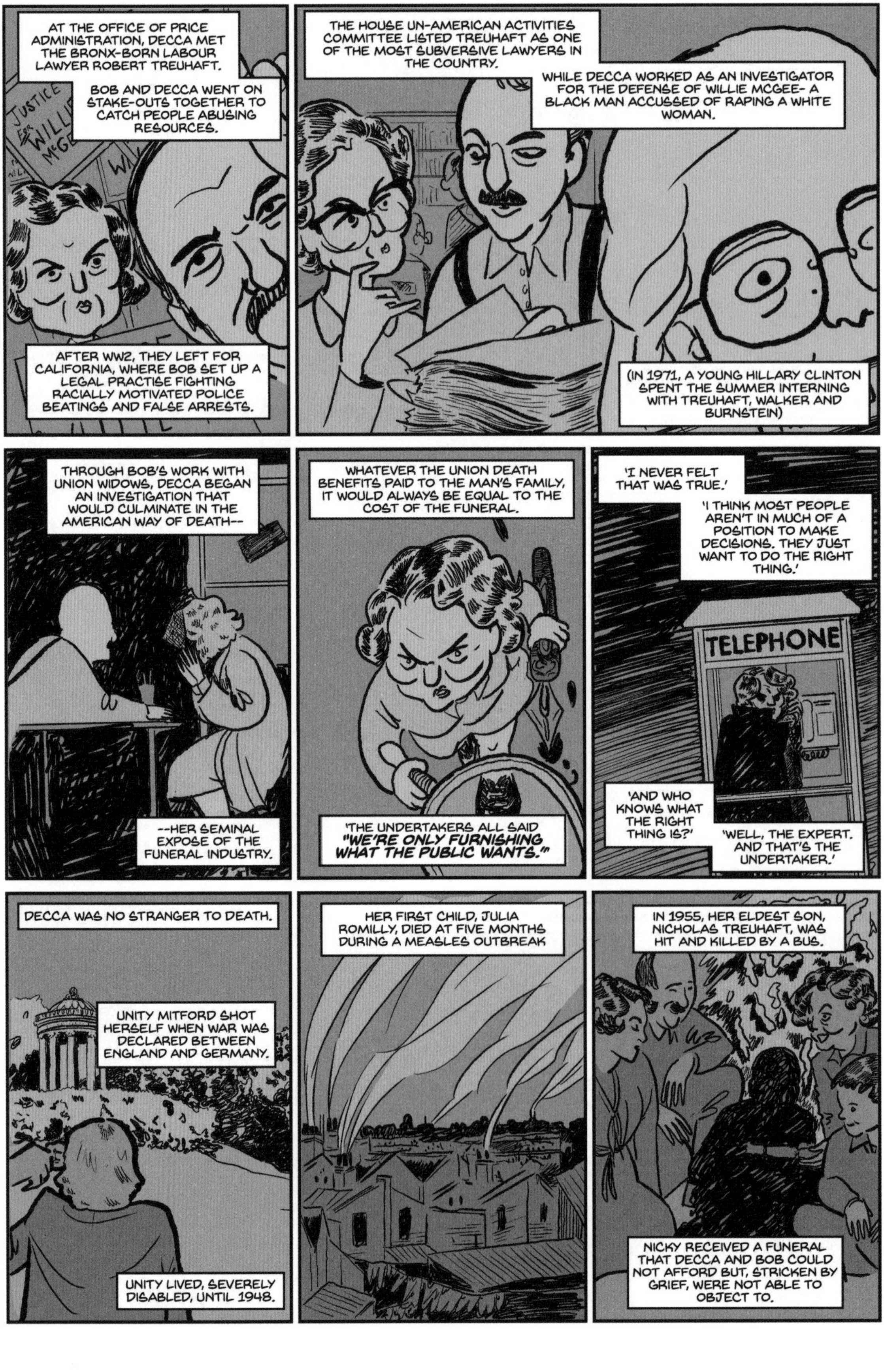

AT THE OFFICE OF PRICE ADMINISTRATION, DECCA MET THE BRONX-BORN LABOUR LAWYER ROBERT TREUHAFT.
BOB AND DECCA WENT ON STAKE-OUTS TOGETHER TO CATCH PEOPLE ABUSING RESOURCES.
JUSTICE FOR WILLIE McGEE
AFTER WW2, THEY LEFT FOR CALIFORNIA, WHERE BOB SET UP A LEGAL PRACTISE FIGHTING RACIALLY MOTIVATED POLICE BEATINGS AND FALSE ARRESTS.
THE HOUSE UN-AMERICAN ACTIVITIES COMMITTEE LISTED TREUHAFT AS ONE OF THE MOST SUBVERSIVE LAWYERS IN THE COUNTRY.
WHILE DECCA WORKED AS AN INVESTIGATOR FOR THE DEFENSE OF WILLIE MCGEE- A BLACK MAN ACCUSSED OF RAPING A WHITE WOMAN.
(IN 1971, A YOUNG HILLARY CLINTON SPENT THE SUMMER INTERNING WITH TREUHAFT, WALKER AND BURNSTEIN)
THROUGH BOB'S WORK WITH UNION WIDOWS, DECCA BEGAN AN INVESTIGATION THAT WOULD CULMINATE IN THE AMERICAN WAY OF DEATH--
--HER SEMINAL EXPOSE OF THE FUNERAL INDUSTRY.
WHATEVER THE UNION DEATH BENEFITS PAID TO THE MAN'S FAMILY, IT WOULD ALWAYS BE EQUAL TO THE COST OF THE FUNERAL.
'THE UNDERTAKERS ALL SAID ***"WE'RE ONLY FURNISHING WHAT THE PUBLIC WANTS."***
'I NEVER FELT THAT WAS TRUE.'
'I THINK MOST PEOPLE AREN'T IN MUCH OF A POSITION TO MAKE DECISIONS. THEY JUST WANT TO DO THE RIGHT THING.'
TELEPHONE
'AND WHO KNOWS WHAT THE RIGHT THING IS?'
'WELL, THE EXPERT. AND THAT'S THE UNDERTAKER.'
DECCA WAS NO STRANGER TO DEATH.
UNITY MITFORD SHOT HERSELF WHEN WAR WAS DECLARED BETWEEN ENGLAND AND GERMANY.
UNITY LIVED, SEVERELY DISABLED, UNTIL 1948.
HER FIRST CHILD, JULIA ROMILLY, DIED AT FIVE MONTHS DURING A MEASLES OUTBREAK
IN 1955, HER ELDEST SON, NICHOLAS TREUHAFT, WAS HIT AND KILLED BY A BUS.
NICKY RECEIVED A FUNERAL THAT DECCA AND BOB COULD NOT AFFORD BUT, STRICKEN BY GRIEF, WERE NOT ABLE TO OBJECT TO.

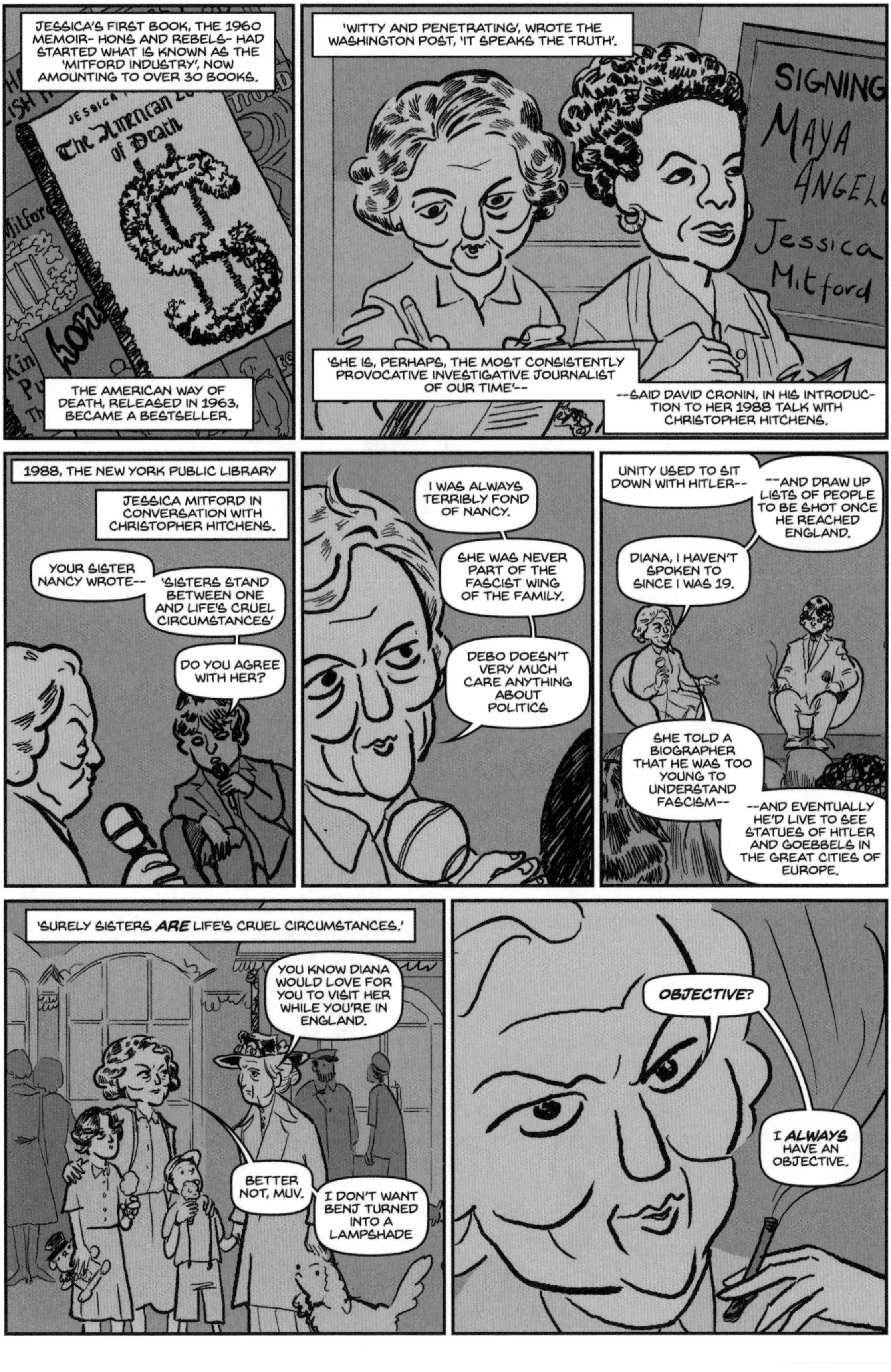
JESSICA'S FIRST BOOK, THE 1960 MEMOIR- HONS AND REBELS- HAD STARTED WHAT IS KNOWN AS THE 'MITFORD INDUSTRY', NOW AMOUNTING TO OVER 30 BOOKS.
The American Way of Death
THE AMERICAN WAY OF DEATH, RELEASED IN 1963, BECAME A BESTSELLER.
'WITTY AND PENETRATING', WROTE THE WASHINGTON POST, 'IT SPEAKS THE TRUTH'.
SIGNING
MAYA ANGEL
Jessica Mitford
'SHE IS, PERHAPS, THE MOST CONSISTENTLY PROVOCATIVE INVESTIGATIVE JOURNALIST OF OUR TIME'--
--SAID DAVID CRONIN, IN HIS INTRODUCTION TO HER 1988 TALK WITH CHRISTOPHER HITCHENS.
1988, THE NEW YORK PUBLIC LIBRARY
JESSICA MITFORD IN CONVERSATION WITH CHRISTOPHER HITCHENS.
YOUR SISTER NANCY WROTE--
'SISTERS STAND BETWEEN ONE AND LIFE'S CRUEL CIRCUMSTANCES'
DO YOU AGREE WITH HER?
I WAS ALWAYS TERRIBLY FOND OF NANCY.
SHE WAS NEVER PART OF THE FASCIST WING OF THE FAMILY.
DEBO DOESN'T VERY MUCH CARE ANYTHING ABOUT POLITICS
UNITY USED TO SIT DOWN WITH HITLER--
--AND DRAW UP LISTS OF PEOPLE TO BE SHOT ONCE HE REACHED ENGLAND.
DIANA, I HAVEN'T SPOKEN TO SINCE I WAS 19.
SHE TOLD A BIOGRAPHER THAT HE WAS TOO YOUNG TO UNDERSTAND FASCISM--
--AND EVENTUALLY HE'D LIVE TO SEE STATUES OF HITLER AND GOEBBELS IN THE GREAT CITIES OF EUROPE.
'SURELY SISTERS ARE LIFE'S CRUEL CIRCUMSTANCES.'
YOU KNOW DIANA WOULD LOVE FOR YOU TO VISIT HER WHILE YOU'RE IN ENGLAND.
BETTER NOT, MUV.
I DON'T WANT BENJ TURNED INTO A LAMPSHADE
OBJECTIVE?
I ALWAYS HAVE AN OBJECTIVE.

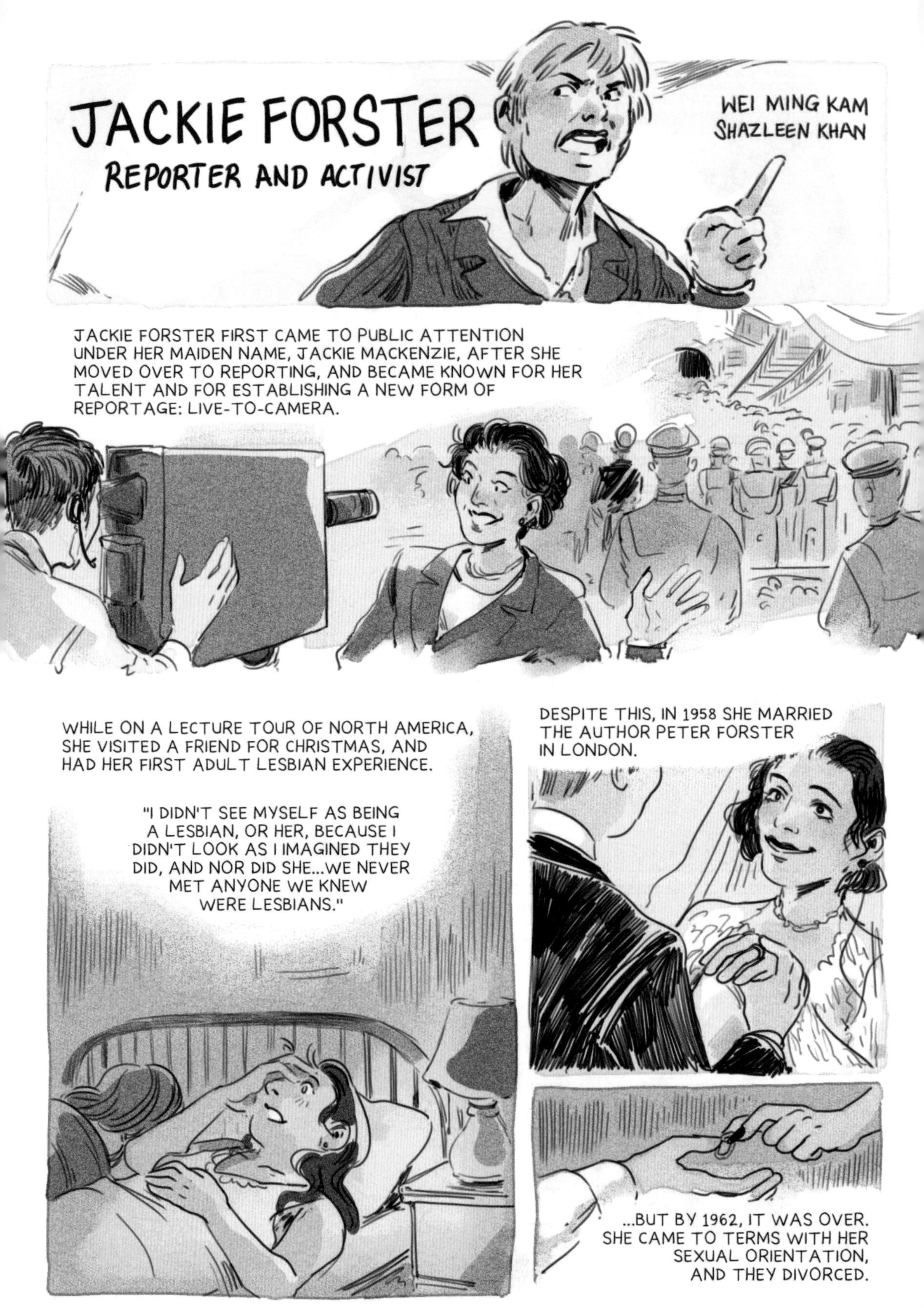
JACKIE FORSTER
REPORTER AND ACTIVIST
WEI MING KAM
SHAZLEEN KHAN
JACKIE FORSTER FIRST CAME TO PUBLIC ATTENTION UNDER HER MAIDEN NAME, JACKIE MACKENZIE, AFTER SHE MOVED OVER TO REPORTING, AND BECAME KNOWN FOR HER TALENT AND FOR ESTABLISHING A NEW FORM OF REPORTAGE: LIVE-TO-CAMERA.
WHILE ON A LECTURE TOUR OF NORTH AMERICA, SHE VISITED A FRIEND FOR CHRISTMAS, AND HAD HER FIRST ADULT LESBIAN EXPERIENCE.
"I DIDN'T SEE MYSELF AS BEING A LESBIAN, OR HER, BECAUSE I DIDN'T LOOK AS I IMAGINED THEY DID, AND NOR DID SHE...WE NEVER MET ANYONE WE KNEW WERE LESBIANS."
DESPITE THIS, IN 1958 SHE MARRIED THE AUTHOR PETER FORSTER IN LONDON.
...BUT BY 1962, IT WAS OVER. SHE CAME TO TERMS WITH HER SEXUAL ORIENTATION, AND THEY DIVORCED.

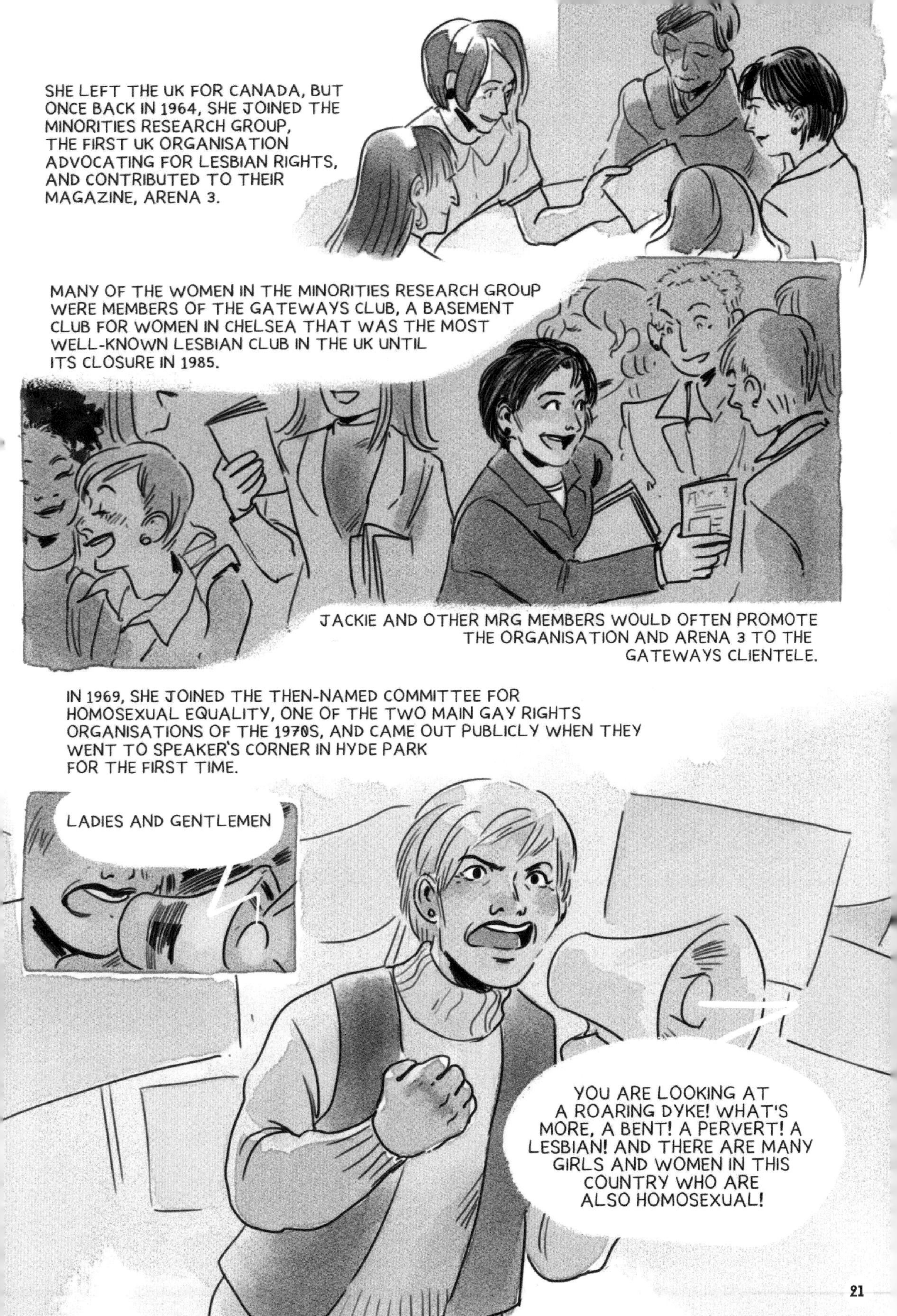
SHE LEFT THE UK FOR CANADA, BUT ONCE BACK IN 1964, SHE JOINED THE MINORITIES RESEARCH GROUP, THE FIRST UK ORGANISATION ADVOCATING FOR LESBIAN RIGHTS, AND CONTRIBUTED TO THEIR MAGAZINE, ARENA 3.
MANY OF THE WOMEN IN THE MINORITIES RESEARCH GROUP WERE MEMBERS OF THE GATEWAYS CLUB, A BASEMENT CLUB FOR WOMEN IN CHELSEA THAT WAS THE MOST WELL-KNOWN LESBIAN CLUB IN THE UK UNTIL ITS CLOSURE IN 1985.
JACKIE AND OTHER MRG MEMBERS WOULD OFTEN PROMOTE THE ORGANISATION AND ARENA 3 TO THE GATEWAYS CLIENTELE.
IN 1969, SHE JOINED THE THEN-NAMED COMMITTEE FOR HOMOSEXUAL EQUALITY, ONE OF THE TWO MAIN GAY RIGHTS ORGANISATIONS OF THE 1970S, AND CAME OUT PUBLICLY WHEN THEY WENT TO SPEAKER'S CORNER IN HYDE PARK FOR THE FIRST TIME.
LADIES AND GENTLEMEN
YOU ARE LOOKING AT A ROARING DYKE! WHAT'S MORE, A BENT! A PERVERT! A LESBIAN! AND THERE ARE MANY GIRLS AND WOMEN IN THIS COUNTRY WHO ARE ALSO HOMOSEXUAL!

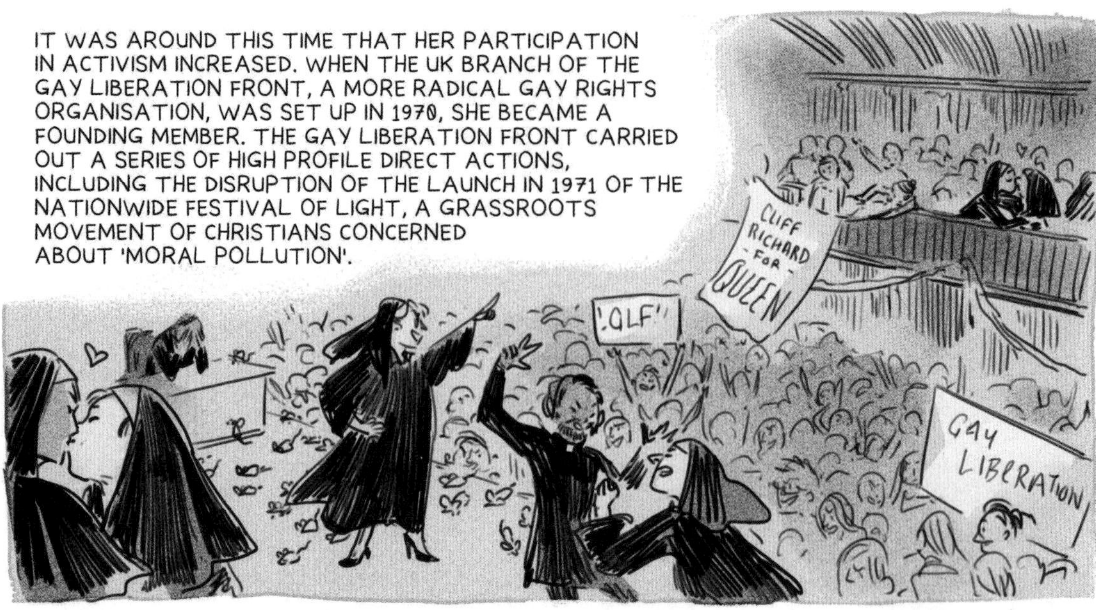
IT WAS AROUND THIS TIME THAT HER PARTICIPATION IN ACTIVISM INCREASED. WHEN THE UK BRANCH OF THE GAY LIBERATION FRONT, A MORE RADICAL GAY RIGHTS ORGANISATION, WAS SET UP IN 1970, SHE BECAME A FOUNDING MEMBER. THE GAY LIBERATION FRONT CARRIED OUT A SERIES OF HIGH PROFILE DIRECT ACTIONS, INCLUDING THE DISRUPTION OF THE LAUNCH IN 1971 OF THE NATIONWIDE FESTIVAL OF LIGHT, A GRASSROOTS MOVEMENT OF CHRISTIANS CONCERNED ABOUT 'MORAL POLLUTION'.
CLIFF RICHARD -FOR- QUEEN
GLF
GAY LIBERATION

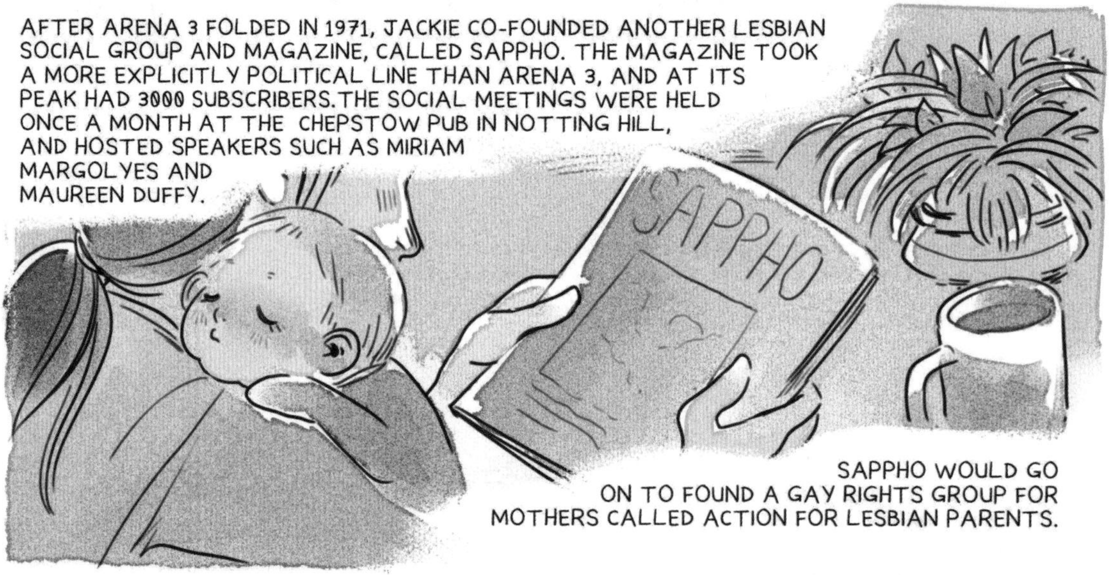
AFTER ARENA 3 FOLDED IN 1971, JACKIE CO-FOUNDED ANOTHER LESBIAN SOCIAL GROUP AND MAGAZINE, CALLED SAPPHO. THE MAGAZINE TOOK A MORE EXPLICITLY POLITICAL LINE THAN ARENA 3, AND AT ITS PEAK HAD 3000 SUBSCRIBERS. THE SOCIAL MEETINGS WERE HELD ONCE A MONTH AT THE CHEPSTOW PUB IN NOTTING HILL, AND HOSTED SPEAKERS SUCH AS MIRIAM MARGOLYES AND MAUREEN DUFFY.
SAPPHO
SAPPHO WOULD GO ON TO FOUND A GAY RIGHTS GROUP FOR MOTHERS CALLED ACTION FOR LESBIAN PARENTS.

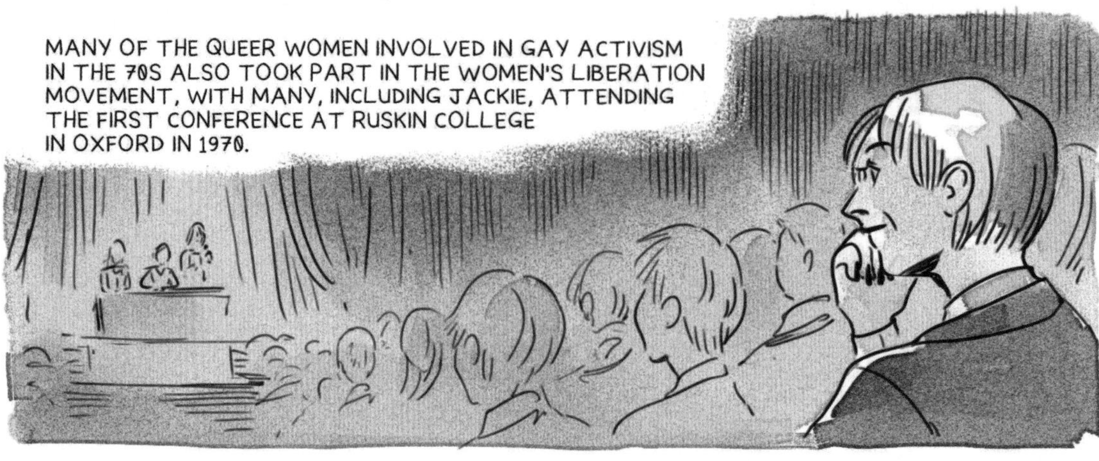
MANY OF THE QUEER WOMEN INVOLVED IN GAY ACTIVISM IN THE 70S ALSO TOOK PART IN THE WOMEN'S LIBERATION MOVEMENT, WITH MANY, INCLUDING JACKIE, ATTENDING THE FIRST CONFERENCE AT RUSKIN COLLEGE IN OXFORD IN 1970.

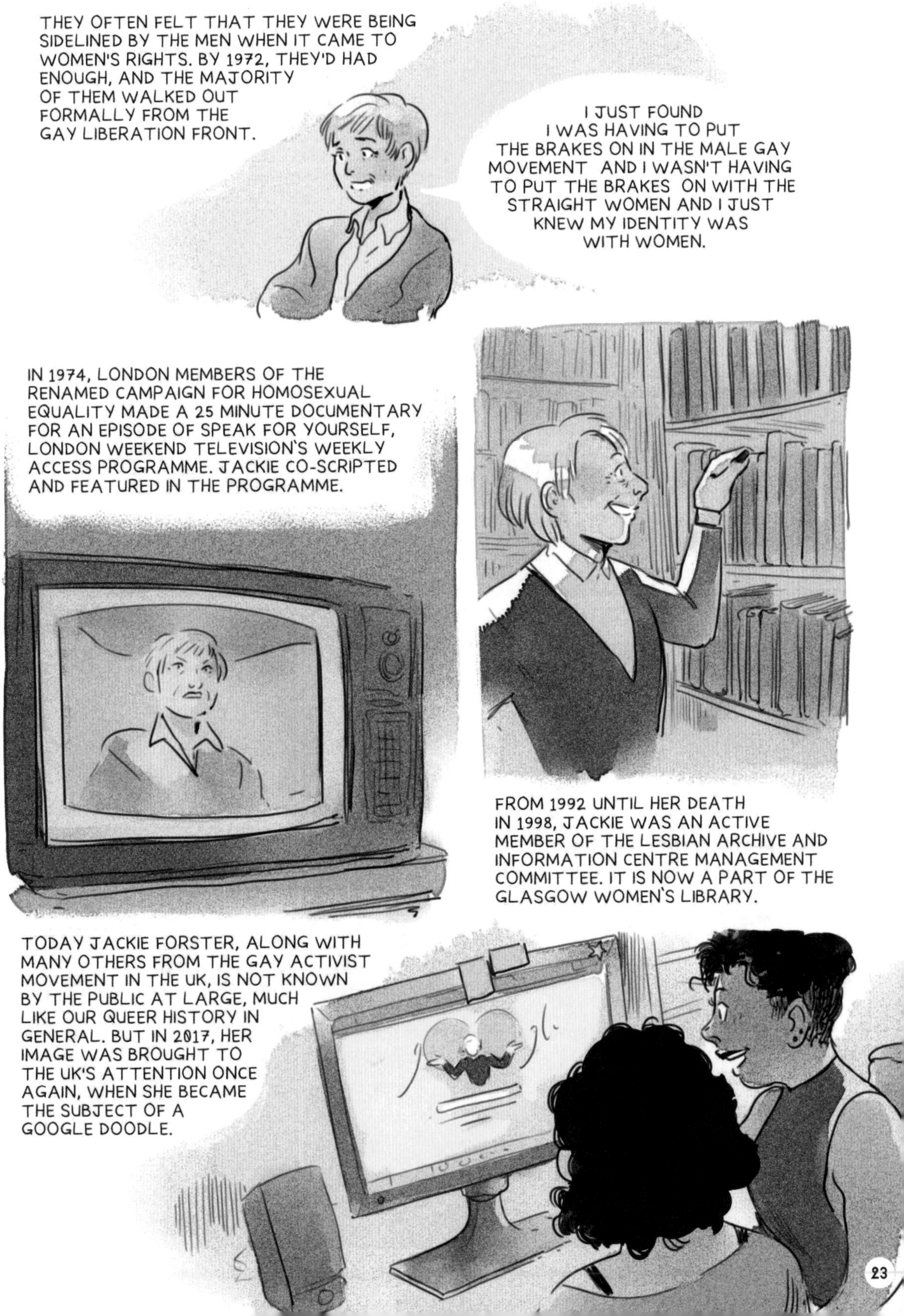
THEY OFTEN FELT THAT THEY WERE BEING SIDELINED BY THE MEN WHEN IT CAME TO WOMEN'S RIGHTS. BY 1972, THEY'D HAD ENOUGH, AND THE MAJORITY OF THEM WALKED OUT FORMALLY FROM THE GAY LIBERATION FRONT.
I JUST FOUND I WAS HAVING TO PUT THE BRAKES ON IN THE MALE GAY MOVEMENT AND I WASN'T HAVING TO PUT THE BRAKES ON WITH THE STRAIGHT WOMEN AND I JUST KNEW MY IDENTITY WAS WITH WOMEN.
IN 1974, LONDON MEMBERS OF THE RENAMED CAMPAIGN FOR HOMOSEXUAL EQUALITY MADE A 25 MINUTE DOCUMENTARY FOR AN EPISODE OF SPEAK FOR YOURSELF, LONDON WEEKEND TELEVISION'S WEEKLY ACCESS PROGRAMME. JACKIE CO-SCRIPTED AND FEATURED IN THE PROGRAMME.
FROM 1992 UNTIL HER DEATH IN 1998, JACKIE WAS AN ACTIVE MEMBER OF THE LESBIAN ARCHIVE AND INFORMATION CENTRE MANAGEMENT COMMITTEE. IT IS NOW A PART OF THE GLASGOW WOMEN'S LIBRARY.
TODAY JACKIE FORSTER, ALONG WITH MANY OTHERS FROM THE GAY ACTIVIST MOVEMENT IN THE UK, IS NOT KNOWN BY THE PUBLIC AT LARGE, MUCH LIKE OUR QUEER HISTORY IN GENERAL. BUT IN 2017, HER IMAGE WAS BROUGHT TO THE UK'S ATTENTION ONCE AGAIN, WHEN SHE BECAME THE SUBJECT OF A GOOGLE DOODLE.

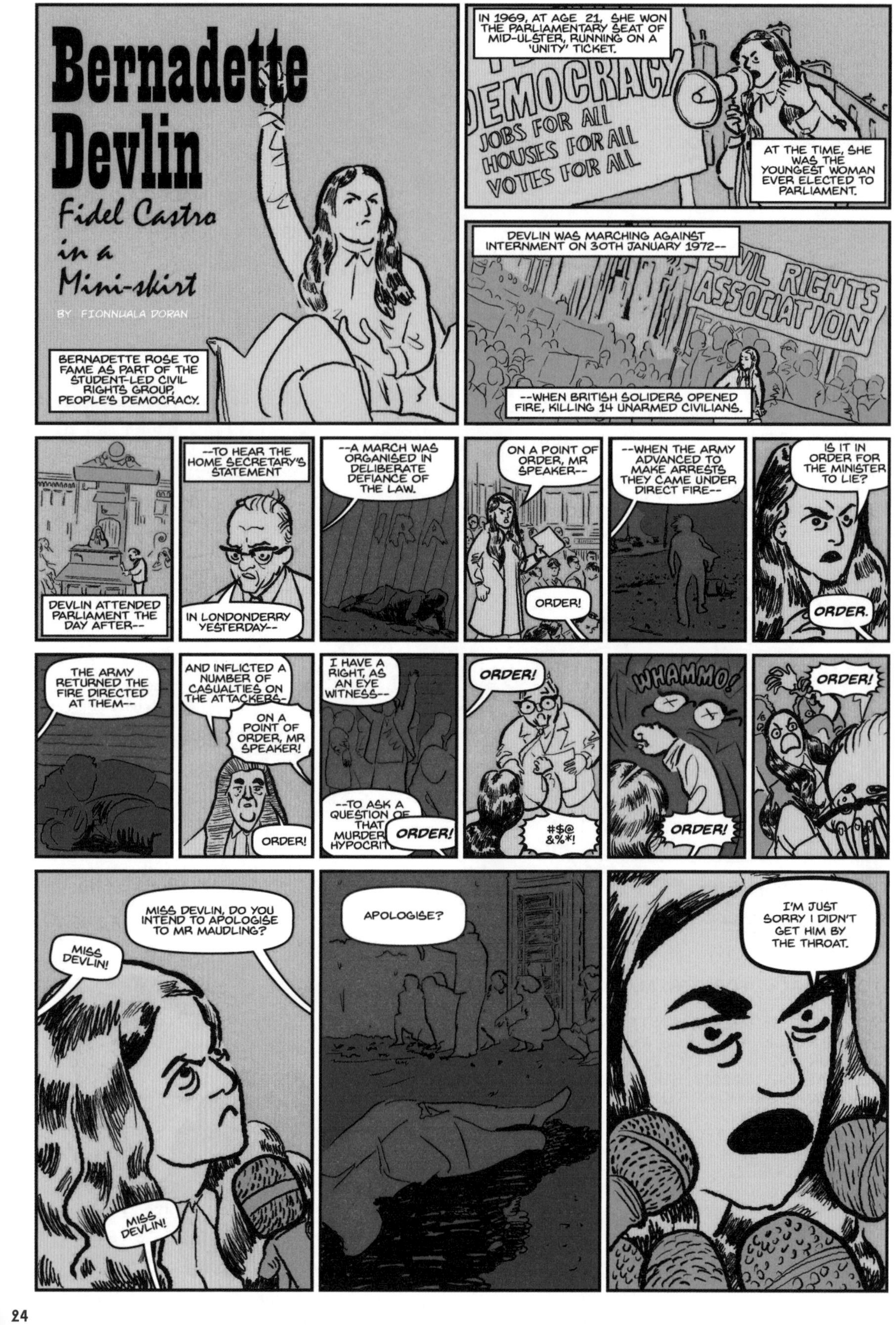
Bernadette Devlin
Fidel Castro in a Mini-skirt
BY FIONNUALA DORAN
BERNADETTE ROSE TO FAME AS PART OF THE STUDENT-LED CIVIL RIGHTS GROUP, PEOPLE'S DEMOCRACY.
IN 1969, AT AGE 21, SHE WON THE PARLIAMENTARY SEAT OF MID-ULSTER, RUNNING ON A 'UNITY' TICKET.
DEMOCRACY
JOBS FOR ALL
HOUSES FOR ALL
VOTES FOR ALL
AT THE TIME, SHE WAS THE YOUNGEST WOMAN EVER ELECTED TO PARLIAMENT.
DEVLIN WAS MARCHING AGAINST INTERNMENT ON 30TH JANUARY 1972--
CIVIL RIGHTS ASSOCIATION
--WHEN BRITISH SOLIDERS OPENED FIRE, KILLING 14 UNARMED CIVILIANS.
DEVLIN ATTENDED PARLIAMENT THE DAY AFTER--
--TO HEAR THE HOME SECRETARY'S STATEMENT
IN LONDONDERRY YESTERDAY--
--A MARCH WAS ORGANISED IN DELIBERATE DEFIANCE OF THE LAW.
IRA
ON A POINT OF ORDER, MR SPEAKER--
ORDER!
--WHEN THE ARMY ADVANCED TO MAKE ARRESTS THEY CAME UNDER DIRECT FIRE--
IS IT IN ORDER FOR THE MINISTER TO LIE?
ORDER.
THE ARMY RETURNED THE FIRE DIRECTED AT THEM--
AND INFLICTED A NUMBER OF CASUALTIES ON THE ATTACKERS-
ON A POINT OF ORDER, MR SPEAKER!
ORDER!
I HAVE A RIGHT, AS AN EYE WITNESS--
--TO ASK A QUESTION OF THAT MURDER
HYPOCRIT
ORDER!
ORDER!
#$@ &%*!
WHAMMO!
ORDER!
ORDER!
MISS DEVLIN, DO YOU INTEND TO APOLOGISE TO MR MAUDLING?
MISS DEVLIN!
MISS DEVLIN!
APOLOGISE?
I'M JUST SORRY I DIDN'T GET HIM BY THE THROAT.

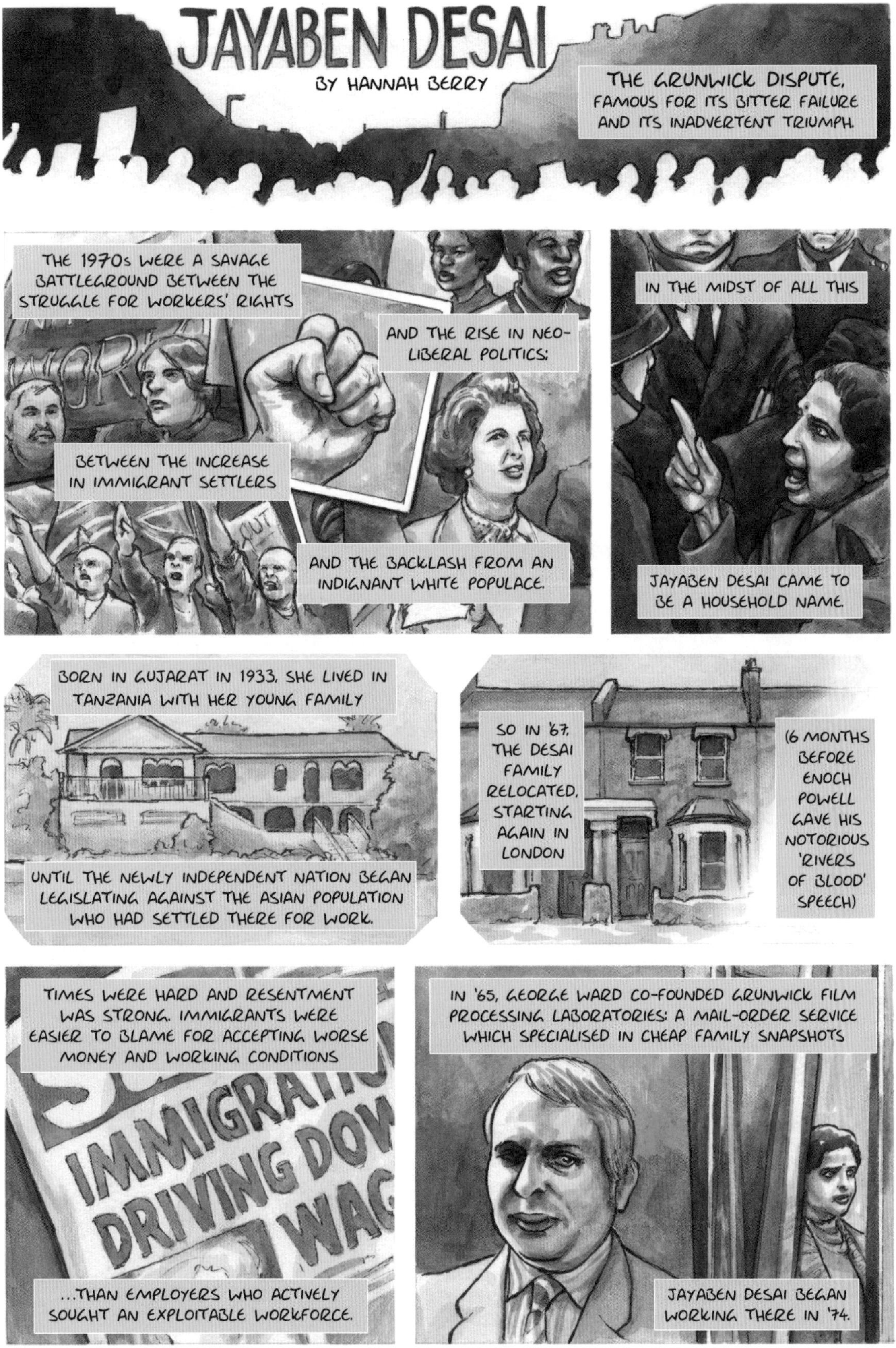
JAYABEN DESAI
BY HANNAH BERRY
THE GRUNWICK DISPUTE, FAMOUS FOR ITS BITTER FAILURE AND ITS INADVERTENT TRIUMPH.
THE 1970s WERE A SAVAGE BATTLEGROUND BETWEEN THE STRUGGLE FOR WORKERS' RIGHTS
AND THE RISE IN NEO-LIBERAL POLITICS;
BETWEEN THE INCREASE IN IMMIGRANT SETTLERS
OUT
AND THE BACKLASH FROM AN INDIGNANT WHITE POPULACE.
IN THE MIDST OF ALL THIS
JAYABEN DESAI CAME TO BE A HOUSEHOLD NAME.
BORN IN GUJARAT IN 1933, SHE LIVED IN TANZANIA WITH HER YOUNG FAMILY
UNTIL THE NEWLY INDEPENDENT NATION BEGAN LEGISLATING AGAINST THE ASIAN POPULATION WHO HAD SETTLED THERE FOR WORK.
SO IN '67, THE DESAI FAMILY RELOCATED, STARTING AGAIN IN LONDON
(6 MONTHS BEFORE ENOCH POWELL GAVE HIS NOTORIOUS 'RIVERS OF BLOOD' SPEECH)
TIMES WERE HARD AND RESENTMENT WAS STRONG. IMMIGRANTS WERE EASIER TO BLAME FOR ACCEPTING WORSE MONEY AND WORKING CONDITIONS
...THAN EMPLOYERS WHO ACTIVELY SOUGHT AN EXPLOITABLE WORKFORCE.
IN '65, GEORGE WARD CO-FOUNDED GRUNWICK FILM PROCESSING LABORATORIES: A MAIL-ORDER SERVICE WHICH SPECIALISED IN CHEAP FAMILY SNAPSHOTS
JAYABEN DESAI BEGAN WORKING THERE IN '74.

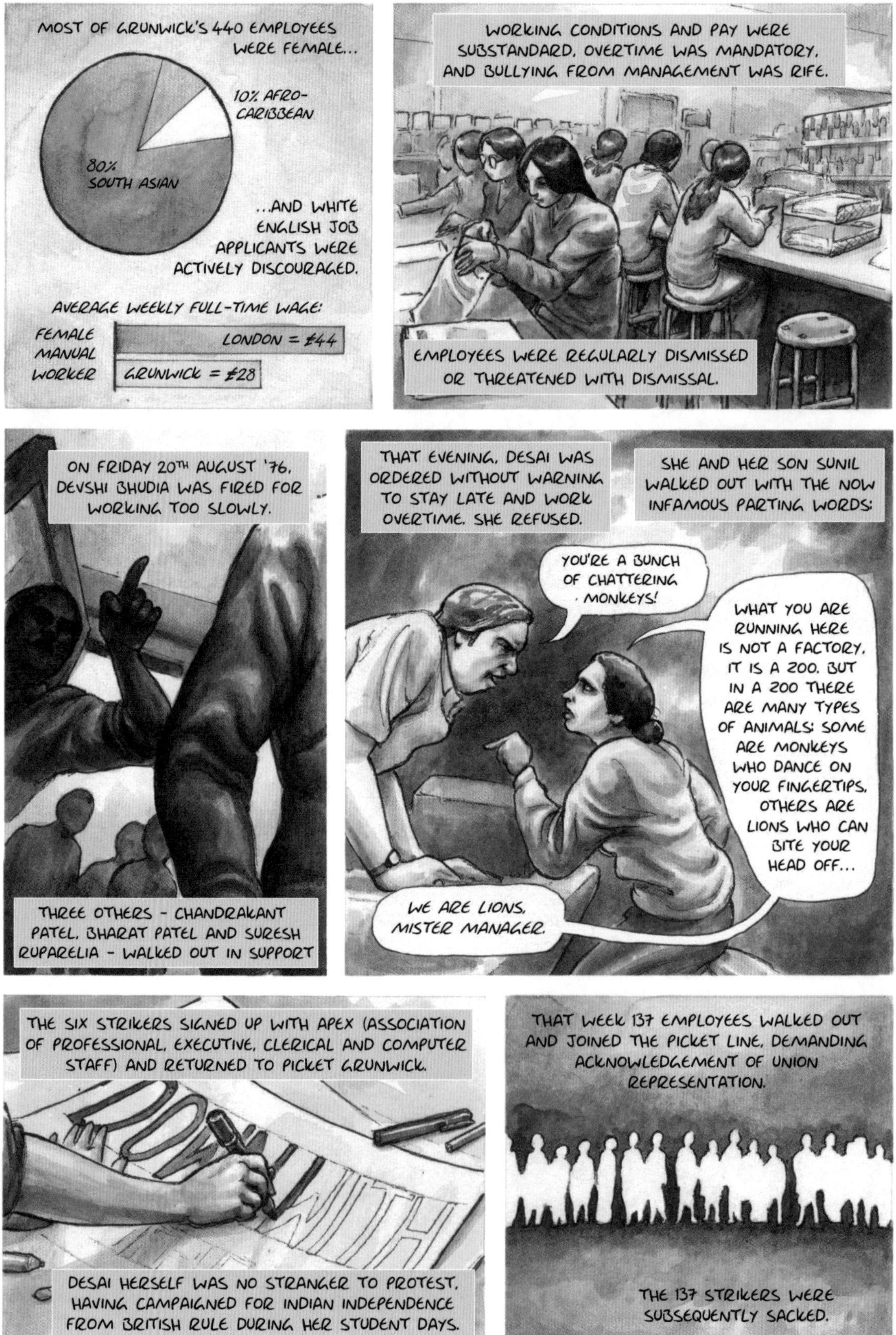
MOST OF GRUNWICK'S 440 EMPLOYEES WERE FEMALE...
10% AFRO-CARIBBEAN
80% SOUTH ASIAN
...AND WHITE ENGLISH JOB APPLICANTS WERE ACTIVELY DISCOURAGED.
AVERAGE WEEKLY FULL-TIME WAGE:
FEMALE MANUAL WORKER
LONDON = £44
GRUNWICK = £28
WORKING CONDITIONS AND PAY WERE SUBSTANDARD, OVERTIME WAS MANDATORY, AND BULLYING FROM MANAGEMENT WAS RIFE.
EMPLOYEES WERE REGULARLY DISMISSED OR THREATENED WITH DISMISSAL.
ON FRIDAY 20TH AUGUST '76, DEVSHI BHUDIA WAS FIRED FOR WORKING TOO SLOWLY.
THREE OTHERS - CHANDRAKANT PATEL, BHARAT PATEL AND SURESH RUPARELIA - WALKED OUT IN SUPPORT
THAT EVENING, DESAI WAS ORDERED WITHOUT WARNING TO STAY LATE AND WORK OVERTIME. SHE REFUSED.
SHE AND HER SON SUNIL WALKED OUT WITH THE NOW INFAMOUS PARTING WORDS:
YOU'RE A BUNCH OF CHATTERING MONKEYS!
WHAT YOU ARE RUNNING HERE IS NOT A FACTORY, IT IS A ZOO. BUT IN A ZOO THERE ARE MANY TYPES OF ANIMALS: SOME ARE MONKEYS WHO DANCE ON YOUR FINGERTIPS, OTHERS ARE LIONS WHO CAN BITE YOUR HEAD OFF...
WE ARE LIONS, MISTER MANAGER.
THE SIX STRIKERS SIGNED UP WITH APEX (ASSOCIATION OF PROFESSIONAL, EXECUTIVE, CLERICAL AND COMPUTER STAFF) AND RETURNED TO PICKET GRUNWICK.
WITH
DESAI HERSELF WAS NO STRANGER TO PROTEST, HAVING CAMPAIGNED FOR INDIAN INDEPENDENCE FROM BRITISH RULE DURING HER STUDENT DAYS.
THAT WEEK 137 EMPLOYEES WALKED OUT AND JOINED THE PICKET LINE, DEMANDING ACKNOWLEDGEMENT OF UNION REPRESENTATION.
THE 137 STRIKERS WERE SUBSEQUENTLY SACKED.

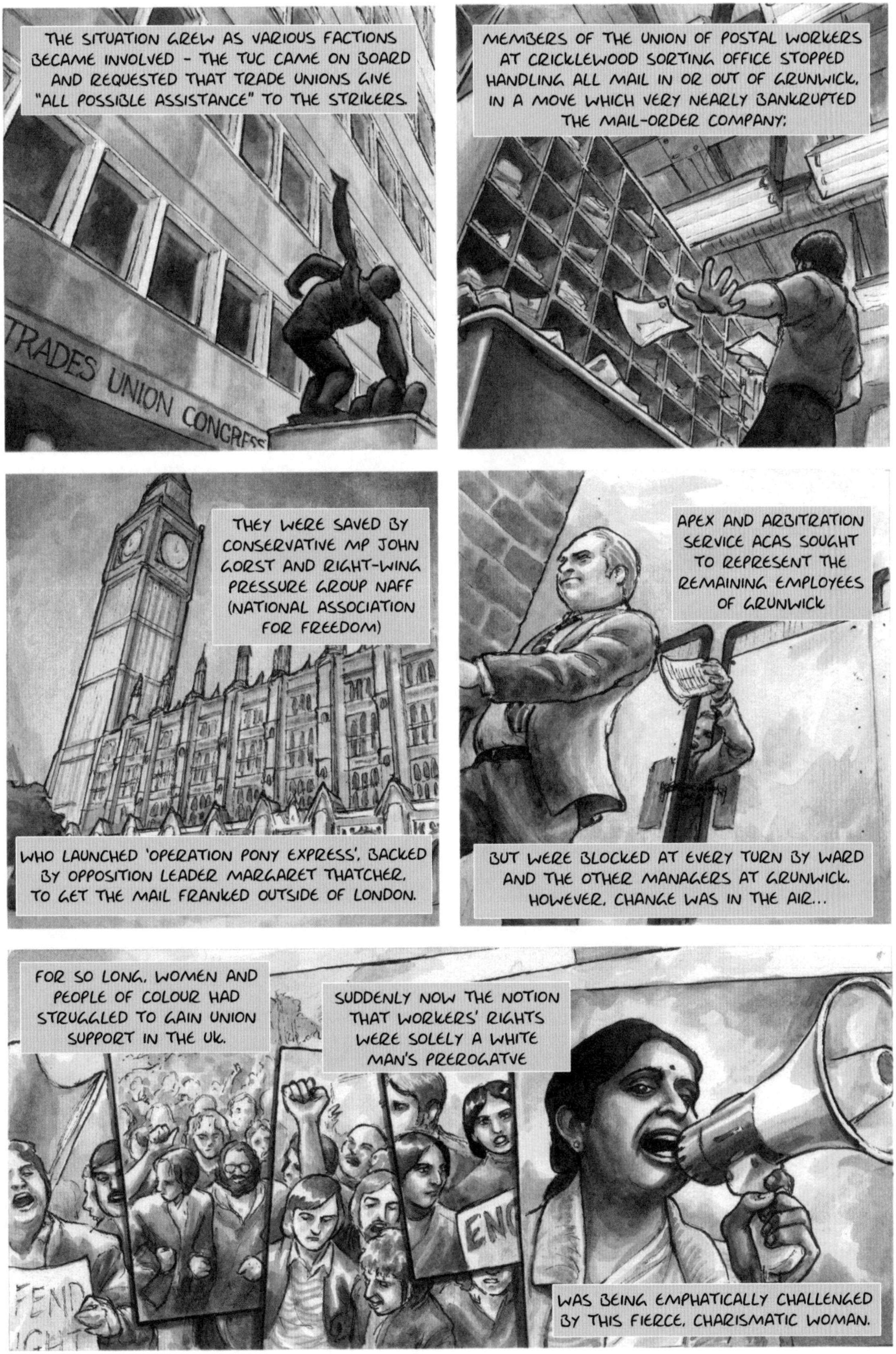
THE SITUATION GREW AS VARIOUS FACTIONS BECAME INVOLVED – THE TUC CAME ON BOARD AND REQUESTED THAT TRADE UNIONS GIVE "ALL POSSIBLE ASSISTANCE" TO THE STRIKERS.
TRADES UNION CONGRES
MEMBERS OF THE UNION OF POSTAL WORKERS AT CRICKLEWOOD SORTING OFFICE STOPPED HANDLING ALL MAIL IN OR OUT OF GRUNWICK, IN A MOVE WHICH VERY NEARLY BANKRUPTED THE MAIL-ORDER COMPANY;
THEY WERE SAVED BY CONSERVATIVE MP JOHN GORST AND RIGHT-WING PRESSURE GROUP NAFF (NATIONAL ASSOCIATION FOR FREEDOM)
WHO LAUNCHED 'OPERATION PONY EXPRESS', BACKED BY OPPOSITION LEADER MARGARET THATCHER, TO GET THE MAIL FRANKED OUTSIDE OF LONDON.
APEX AND ARBITRATION SERVICE ACAS SOUGHT TO REPRESENT THE REMAINING EMPLOYEES OF GRUNWICK
BUT WERE BLOCKED AT EVERY TURN BY WARD AND THE OTHER MANAGERS AT GRUNWICK. HOWEVER, CHANGE WAS IN THE AIR...
FOR SO LONG, WOMEN AND PEOPLE OF COLOUR HAD STRUGGLED TO GAIN UNION SUPPORT IN THE UK.
SUDDENLY NOW THE NOTION THAT WORKERS' RIGHTS WERE SOLELY A WHITE MAN'S PREROGATVE
WAS BEING EMPHATICALLY CHALLENGED BY THIS FIERCE, CHARISMATIC WOMAN.

INCREASING SUPPORT FOR THE 'STRIKERS IN SARIS' LED TO MASS PICKETING IN SUMMER '77 AS SYMPATHETIC PARTIES AND UNION MEMBERS NATIONWIDE JOINED THE PROTEST

ON 11TH JUNE THE NUMBERS PEAKED AT AROUND 20,000 SUPPORTERS

AT THE VANGUARD, ARTHUR SCARGILL.

THE METROPOLITAN POLICE DEPLOYED THE NOTORIOUS 'SPECIAL PATROL GROUP' IN RESPONSE.

THERE WERE HUGE NUMBERS OF ARRESTS (500 IN TOTAL) AND CASUALTIES.

ON A SINGLE DAY IN NOVEMBER '77 WHEN 8,000 SUPPORTERS TURNED OUT TO PROTEST, 243 PICKETERS HAD TO BE TREATED FOR INJURIES, 12 OF WHICH WERE FOR BROKEN BONES.

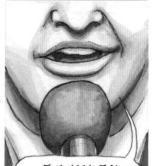

THE MEDIA REVELLED IN THE CARNAGE. THE MASS-PICKETS WERE GLEEFULLY REFERRED TO AS THE "ASCOT OF THE LEFT"

...IT IS ESSENTIAL TO BE SEEN HERE, BEST OF ALL TO GET ARRESTED!

HOWEVER, PICKETING WAS PAUSED IN MID-JULY '77 TO AWAIT THE INQUIRY COMMISSIONED UNDER LORD SCARMAN BY THE LABOUR GOVERNMENT.

AT THE TIME LABOUR WAS IN A PRECARIOUS POSITION WITH A SLIM MAJORITY, AS THE UNIONS WERE ALL TOO AWARE

A LABOUR GOVERNMENT PROVIDED THEM WITH POLITICAL SUPPORT AND A SEAT AT THE TABLE

AND A STRIKE OF THIS MAGNITUDE WAS EXTREMELY DAMAGING.

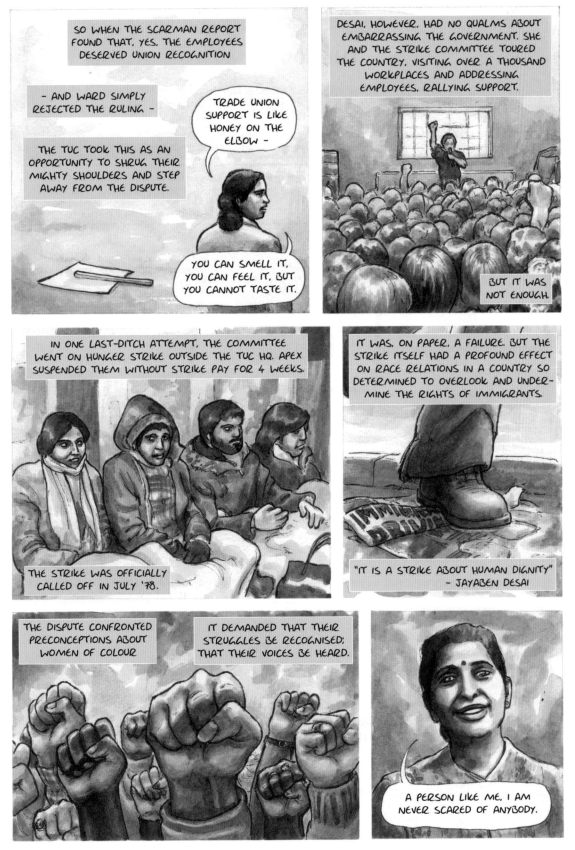

SO WHEN THE SCARMAN REPORT FOUND THAT, YES, THE EMPLOYEES DESERVED UNION RECOGNITION

- AND WARD SIMPLY REJECTED THE RULING -

THE TUC TOOK THIS AS AN OPPORTUNITY TO SHRUG THEIR MIGHTY SHOULDERS AND STEP AWAY FROM THE DISPUTE.

TRADE UNION SUPPORT IS LIKE HONEY ON THE ELBOW -

YOU CAN SMELL IT, YOU CAN FEEL IT, BUT YOU CANNOT TASTE IT.

DESAI, HOWEVER, HAD NO QUALMS ABOUT EMBARRASSING THE GOVERNMENT. SHE AND THE STRIKE COMMITTEE TOURED THE COUNTRY, VISITING OVER A THOUSAND WORKPLACES AND ADDRESSING EMPLOYEES, RALLYING SUPPORT.

BUT IT WAS NOT ENOUGH.

IN ONE LAST-DITCH ATTEMPT, THE COMMITTEE WENT ON HUNGER STRIKE OUTSIDE THE TUC HQ. APEX SUSPENDED THEM WITHOUT STRIKE PAY FOR 4 WEEKS.

THE STRIKE WAS OFFICIALLY CALLED OFF IN JULY '78.

IT WAS, ON PAPER, A FAILURE. BUT THE STRIKE ITSELF HAD A PROFOUND EFFECT ON RACE RELATIONS IN A COUNTRY SO DETERMINED TO OVERLOOK AND UNDER-MINE THE RIGHTS OF IMMIGRANTS.

"IT IS A STRIKE ABOUT HUMAN DIGNITY" - JAYABEN DESAI

THE DISPUTE CONFRONTED PRECONCEPTIONS ABOUT WOMEN OF COLOUR

IT DEMANDED THAT THEIR STRUGGLES BE RECOGNISED; THAT THEIR VOICES BE HEARD.

A PERSON LIKE ME, I AM NEVER SCARED OF ANYBODY.

29

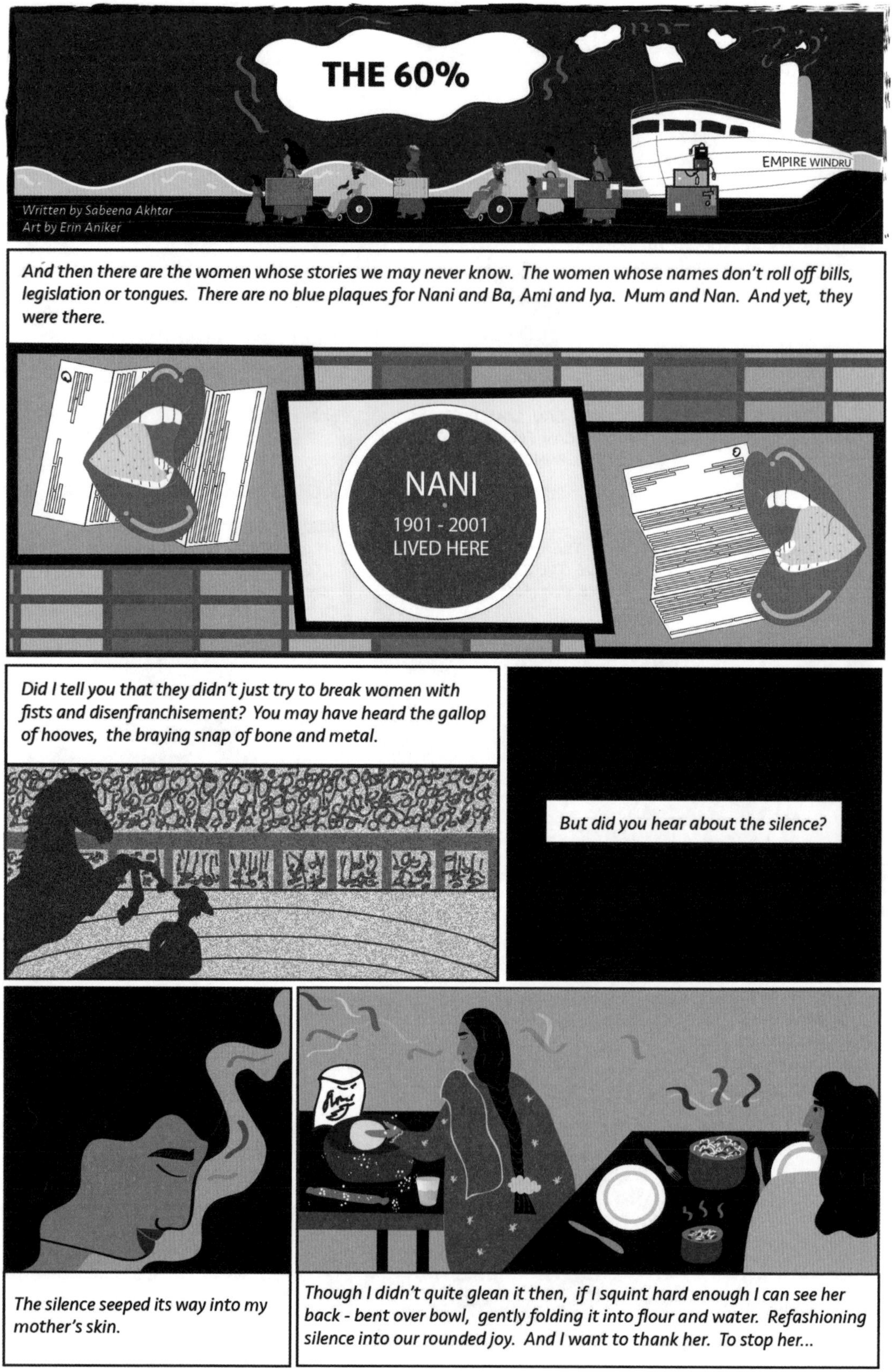
THE 60%
EMPIRE WINDRU
Written by Sabeena Akhtar
Art by Erin Aniker
And then there are the women whose stories we may never know. The women whose names don't roll off bills, legislation or tongues. There are no blue plaques for Nani and Ba, Ami and Iya. Mum and Nan. And yet, they were there.
NANI
1901 - 2001
LIVED HERE
Did I tell you that they didn't just try to break women with fists and disenfranchisement? You may have heard the gallop of hooves, the braying snap of bone and metal.
But did you hear about the silence?
The silence seeped its way into my mother's skin.
Though I didn't quite glean it then, if I squint hard enough I can see her back - bent over bowl, gently folding it into flour and water. Refashioning silence into our rounded joy. And I want to thank her. To stop her...

to scoop her up in my arms and celebrate her. But I didn't. I don't. My grandmother fell through a gap in your map and clawed her way out. But you will not read her name or hear of her strength. She is gone.

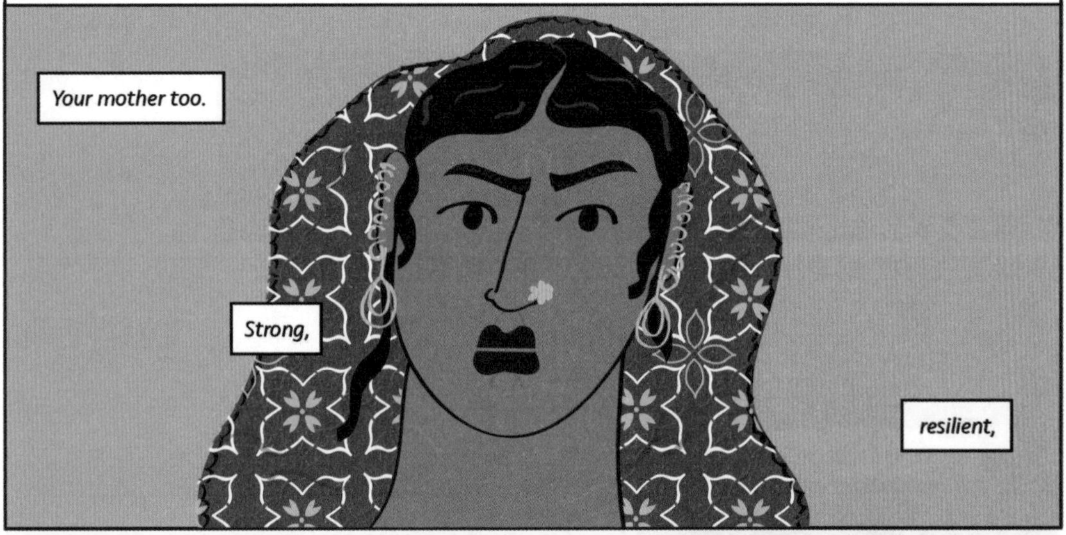
Your mother too.
Strong,
resilient,

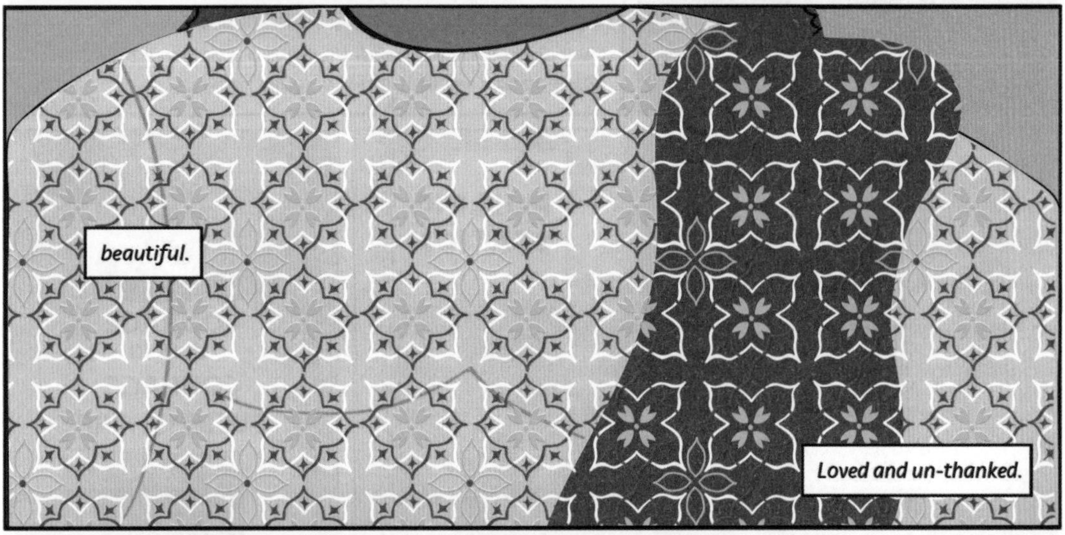
beautiful.
Loved and un-thanked.

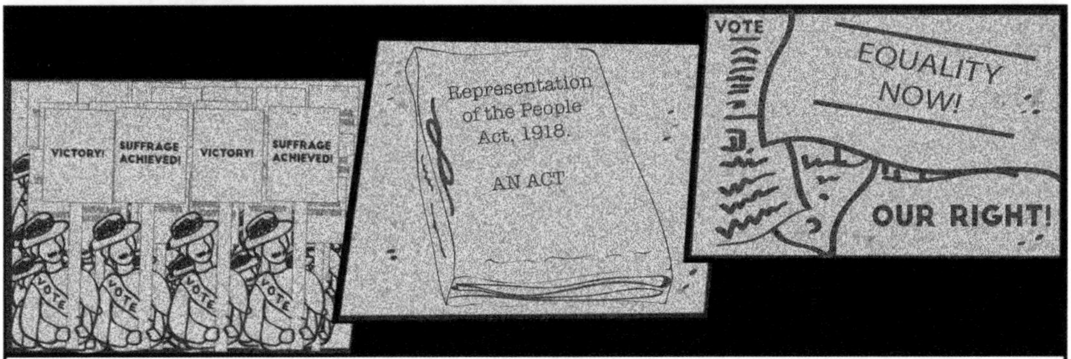
VICTORY!
SUFFRAGE ACHIEVED!
VICTORY!
SUFFRAGE ACHIEVED!
VOTE
VOTE
VOTE
VOTE
Representation of the People Act, 1918.
AN ACT
VOTE
EQUALITY NOW!
OUR RIGHT!

We won't speak about that now. It is not the place, of course. Instead, we will celebrate the victories. (And rightly so.) They were hard won, by women who fought with courage and life. By lobbying and lawlessness. Reformists and suffrage achieved the unthinkable: The Representation of the People Act.

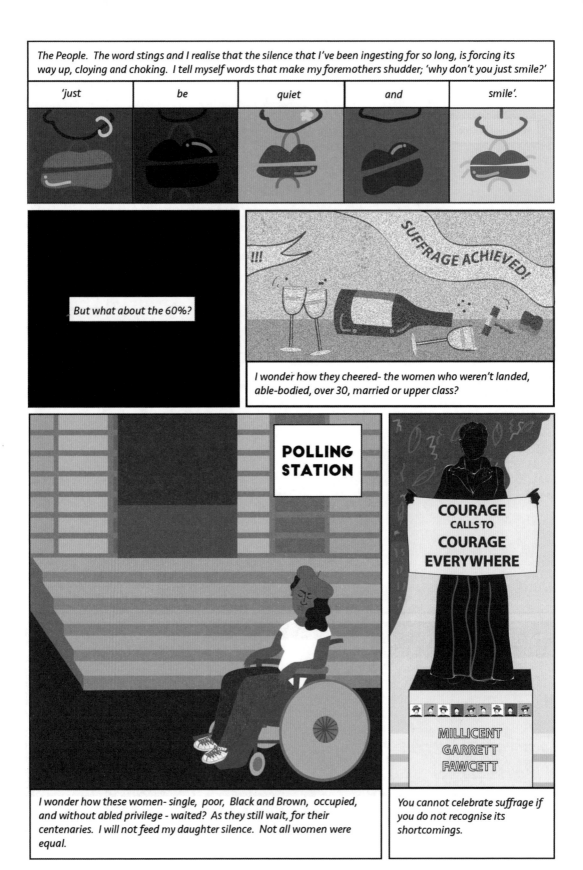

The People. The word stings and I realise that the silence that I've been ingesting for so long, is forcing its way up, cloying and choking. I tell myself words that make my foremothers shudder; 'why don't you just smile?'

'just | be | quiet | and | smile'.

But what about the 60%?

SUFFRAGE ACHIEVED!

!!!

I wonder how they cheered- the women who weren't landed, able-bodied, over 30, married or upper class?

POLLING STATION

COURAGE CALLS TO COURAGE EVERYWHERE

MILLICENT GARRETT FAWCETT

I wonder how these women- single, poor, Black and Brown, occupied, and without abled privilege - waited? As they still wait, for their centenaries. I will not feed my daughter silence. Not all women were equal.

You cannot celebrate suffrage if you do not recognise its shortcomings.

Amidst the swell of chants, our foremothers too made change. They soared, thrived and struggled. Not all had the privilege to fight and franchise. But they were there. In hostile lands with quiet reserve, steel of nerve. They persevered. With aching backs and tired limbs.

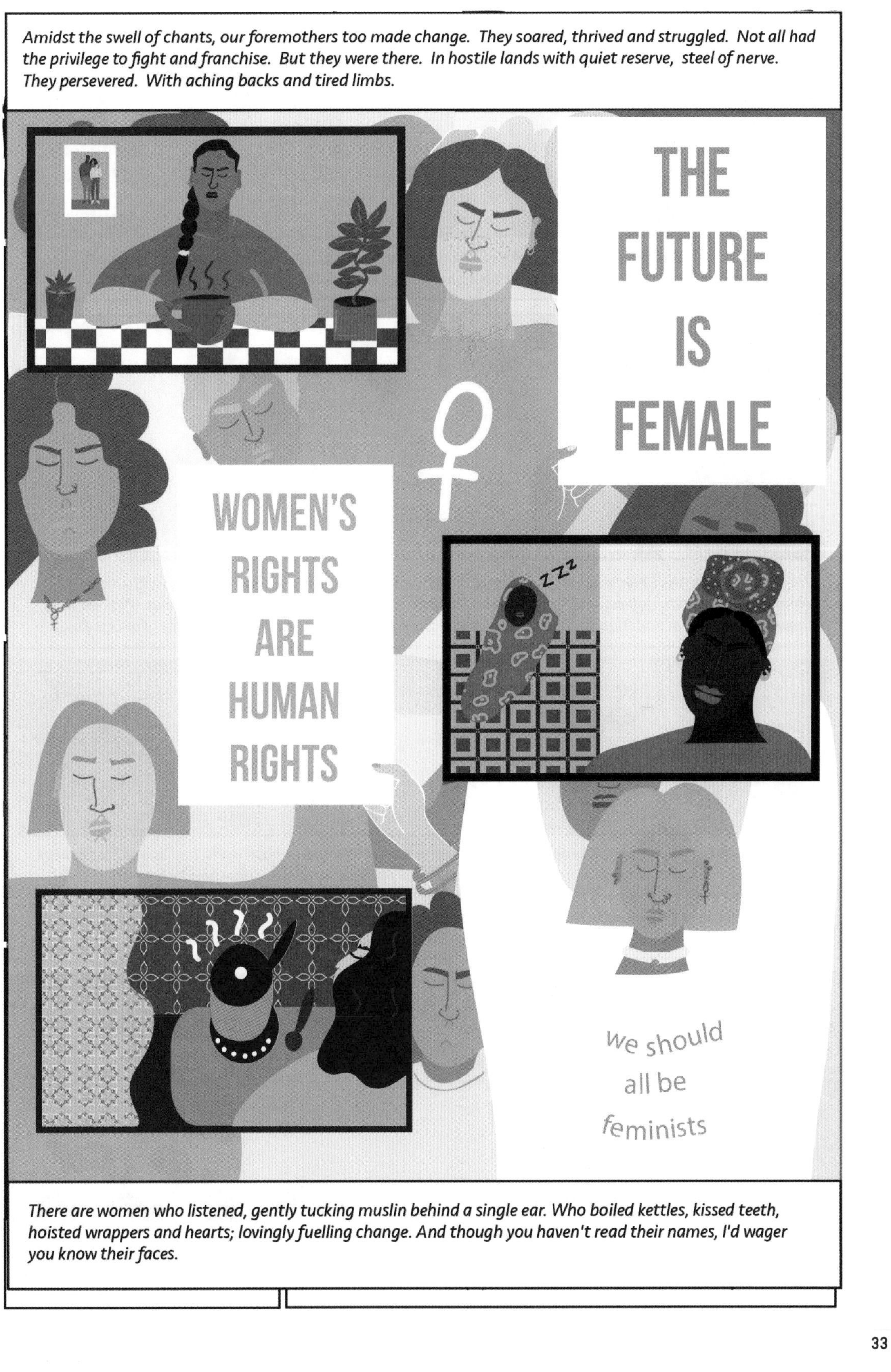
THE FUTURE IS FEMALE
WOMEN'S RIGHTS ARE HUMAN RIGHTS
ZZZ
we should all be feminists

There are women who listened, gently tucking muslin behind a single ear. Who boiled kettles, kissed teeth, hoisted wrappers and hearts; lovingly fuelling change. And though you haven't read their names, I'd wager you know their faces.

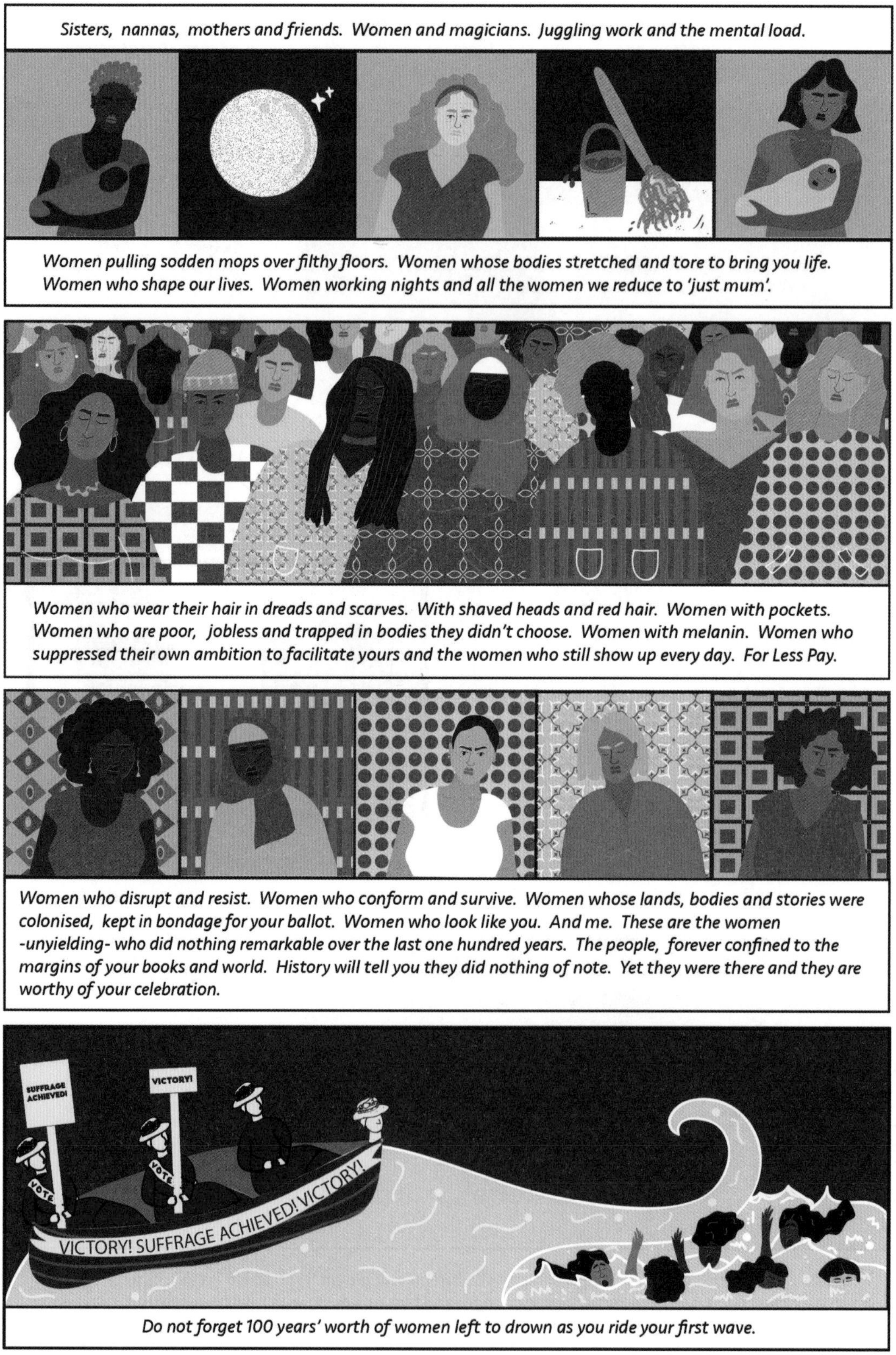
Sisters, nannas, mothers and friends. Women and magicians. Juggling work and the mental load.
Women pulling sodden mops over filthy floors. Women whose bodies stretched and tore to bring you life. Women who shape our lives. Women working nights and all the women we reduce to 'just mum'.
Women who wear their hair in dreads and scarves. With shaved heads and red hair. Women with pockets. Women who are poor, jobless and trapped in bodies they didn't choose. Women with melanin. Women who suppressed their own ambition to facilitate yours and the women who still show up every day. For Less Pay.
Women who disrupt and resist. Women who conform and survive. Women whose lands, bodies and stories were colonised, kept in bondage for your ballot. Women who look like you. And me. These are the women -unyielding- who did nothing remarkable over the last one hundred years. The people, forever confined to the margins of your books and world. History will tell you they did nothing of note. Yet they were there and they are worthy of your celebration.
SUFFRAGE ACHIEVED!
VICTORY!
VOTE
VOTE
VICTORY! SUFFRAGE ACHIEVED! VICTORY!
Do not forget 100 years' worth of women left to drown as you ride your first wave.

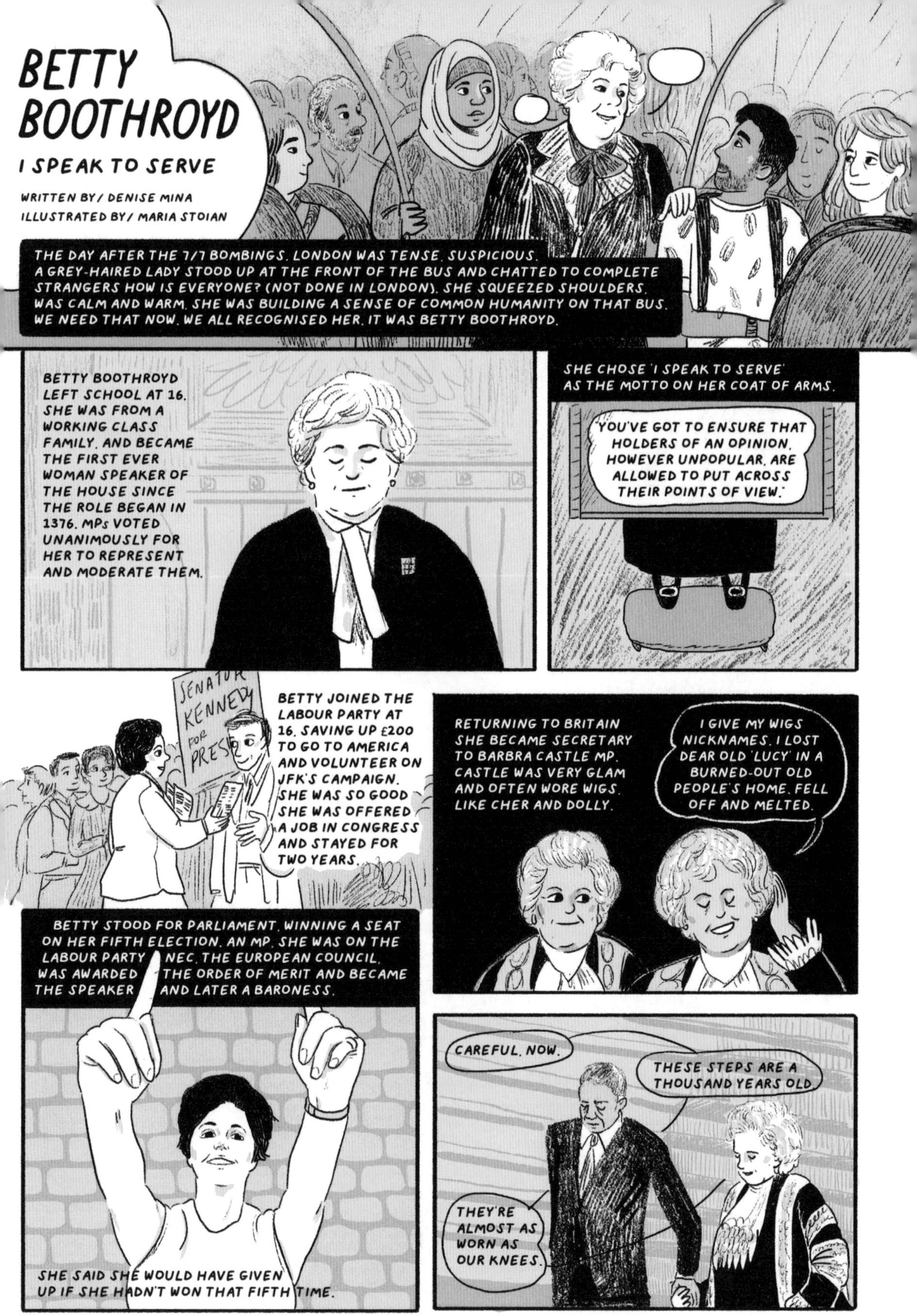
BETTY BOOTHROYD
I SPEAK TO SERVE
WRITTEN BY/ DENISE MINA
ILLUSTRATED BY/ MARIA STOIAN
THE DAY AFTER THE 7/7 BOMBINGS. LONDON WAS TENSE, SUSPICIOUS. A GREY-HAIRED LADY STOOD UP AT THE FRONT OF THE BUS AND CHATTED TO COMPLETE STRANGERS HOW IS EVERYONE? (NOT DONE IN LONDON). SHE SQUEEZED SHOULDERS, WAS CALM AND WARM. SHE WAS BUILDING A SENSE OF COMMON HUMANITY ON THAT BUS. WE NEED THAT NOW. WE ALL RECOGNISED HER. IT WAS BETTY BOOTHROYD.
BETTY BOOTHROYD LEFT SCHOOL AT 16. SHE WAS FROM A WORKING CLASS FAMILY, AND BECAME THE FIRST EVER WOMAN SPEAKER OF THE HOUSE SINCE THE ROLE BEGAN IN 1376. MPs VOTED UNANIMOUSLY FOR HER TO REPRESENT AND MODERATE THEM.
SHE CHOSE 'I SPEAK TO SERVE' AS THE MOTTO ON HER COAT OF ARMS.
'YOU'VE GOT TO ENSURE THAT HOLDERS OF AN OPINION, HOWEVER UNPOPULAR, ARE ALLOWED TO PUT ACROSS THEIR POINTS OF VIEW.'
SENATOR KENNEDY FOR PRES
BETTY JOINED THE LABOUR PARTY AT 16. SAVING UP £200 TO GO TO AMERICA AND VOLUNTEER ON JFK'S CAMPAIGN. SHE WAS SO GOOD SHE WAS OFFERED A JOB IN CONGRESS AND STAYED FOR TWO YEARS.
RETURNING TO BRITAIN SHE BECAME SECRETARY TO BARBRA CASTLE MP. CASTLE WAS VERY GLAM AND OFTEN WORE WIGS, LIKE CHER AND DOLLY.
I GIVE MY WIGS NICKNAMES. I LOST DEAR OLD 'LUCY' IN A BURNED-OUT OLD PEOPLE'S HOME. FELL OFF AND MELTED.
BETTY STOOD FOR PARLIAMENT, WINNING A SEAT ON HER FIFTH ELECTION. AN MP, SHE WAS ON THE LABOUR PARTY NEC, THE EUROPEAN COUNCIL, WAS AWARDED THE ORDER OF MERIT AND BECAME THE SPEAKER AND LATER A BARONESS.
SHE SAID SHE WOULD HAVE GIVEN UP IF SHE HADN'T WON THAT FIFTH TIME.
CAREFUL, NOW.
THESE STEPS ARE A THOUSAND YEARS OLD.
THEY'RE ALMOST AS WORN AS OUR KNEES.

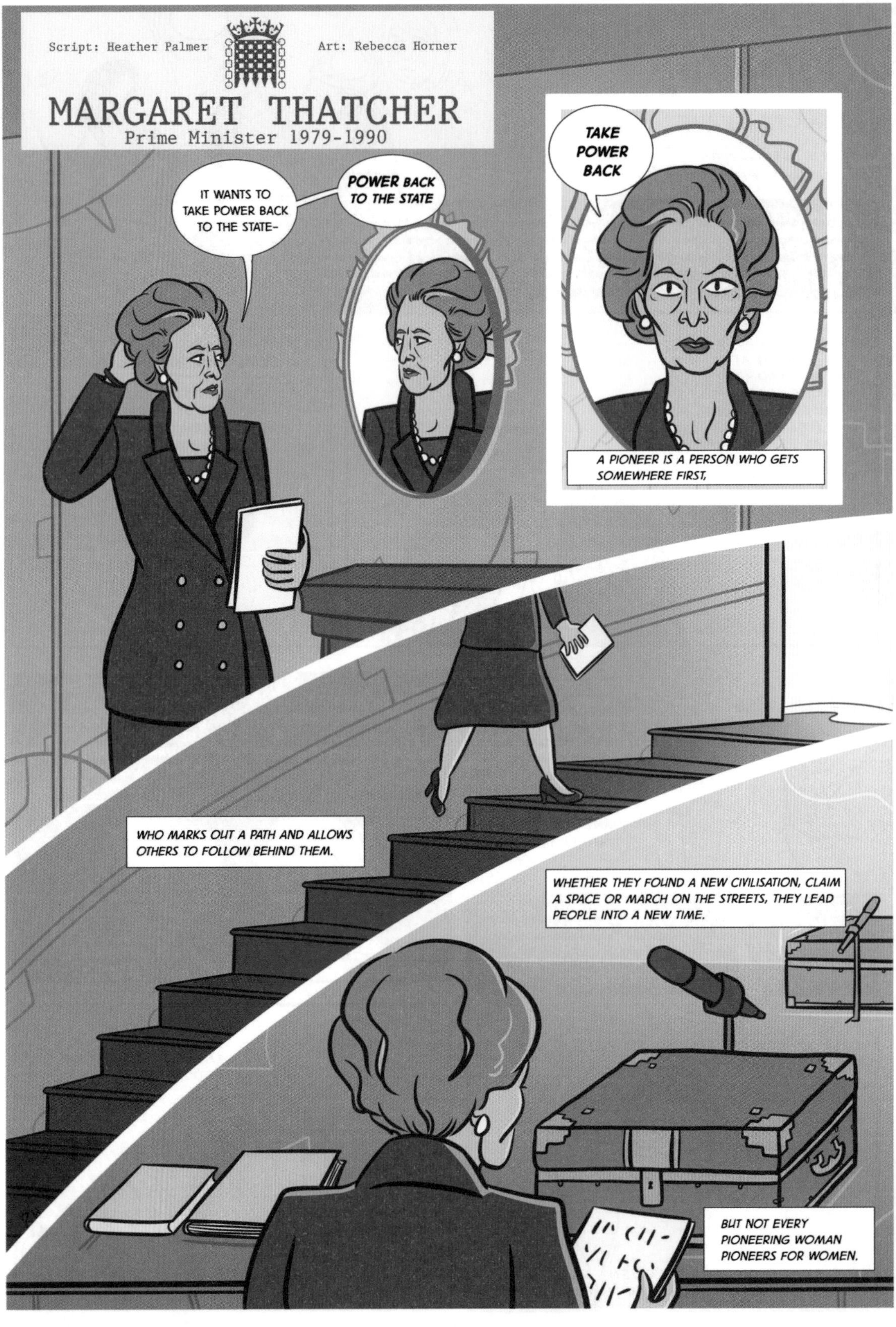
Script: Heather Palmer
Art: Rebecca Horner
MARGARET THATCHER
Prime Minister 1979-1990
IT WANTS TO TAKE POWER BACK TO THE STATE-
POWER BACK TO THE STATE
TAKE POWER BACK
A PIONEER IS A PERSON WHO GETS SOMEWHERE FIRST,
WHO MARKS OUT A PATH AND ALLOWS OTHERS TO FOLLOW BEHIND THEM.
WHETHER THEY FOUND A NEW CIVILISATION, CLAIM A SPACE OR MARCH ON THE STREETS, THEY LEAD PEOPLE INTO A NEW TIME.
BUT NOT EVERY PIONEERING WOMAN PIONEERS FOR WOMEN.

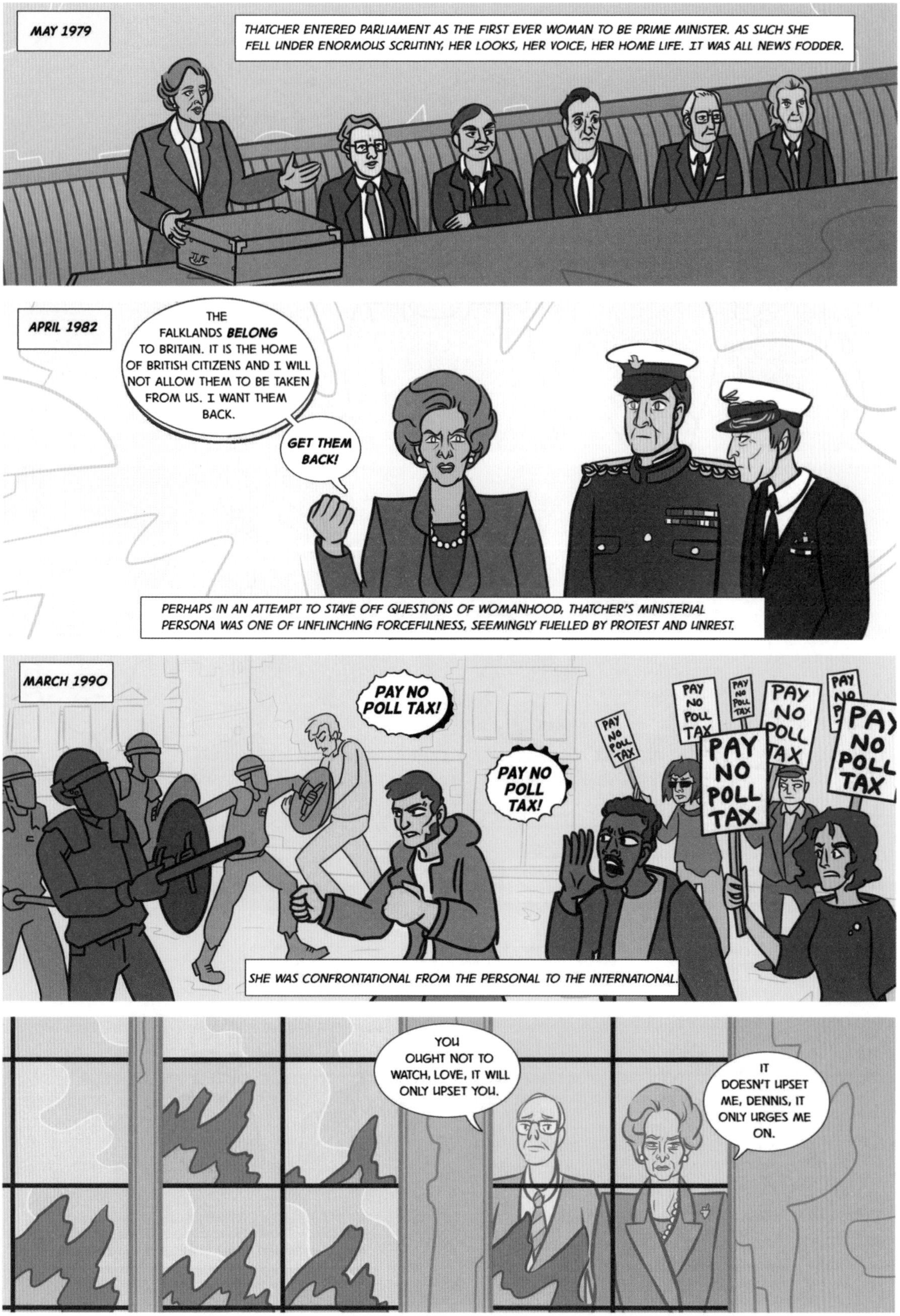
MAY 1979
THATCHER ENTERED PARLIAMENT AS THE FIRST EVER WOMAN TO BE PRIME MINISTER. AS SUCH SHE FELL UNDER ENORMOUS SCRUTINY, HER LOOKS, HER VOICE, HER HOME LIFE. IT WAS ALL NEWS FODDER.
APRIL 1982
THE FALKLANDS BELONG TO BRITAIN. IT IS THE HOME OF BRITISH CITIZENS AND I WILL NOT ALLOW THEM TO BE TAKEN FROM US. I WANT THEM BACK.
GET THEM BACK!
PERHAPS IN AN ATTEMPT TO STAVE OFF QUESTIONS OF WOMANHOOD, THATCHER'S MINISTERIAL PERSONA WAS ONE OF UNFLINCHING FORCEFULNESS, SEEMINGLY FUELLED BY PROTEST AND UNREST.
MARCH 1990
PAY NO POLL TAX!
PAY NO POLL TAX!
PAY NO POLL TAX
SHE WAS CONFRONTATIONAL FROM THE PERSONAL TO THE INTERNATIONAL.
YOU OUGHT NOT TO WATCH, LOVE, IT WILL ONLY UPSET YOU.
IT DOESN'T UPSET ME, DENNIS, IT ONLY URGES ME ON.

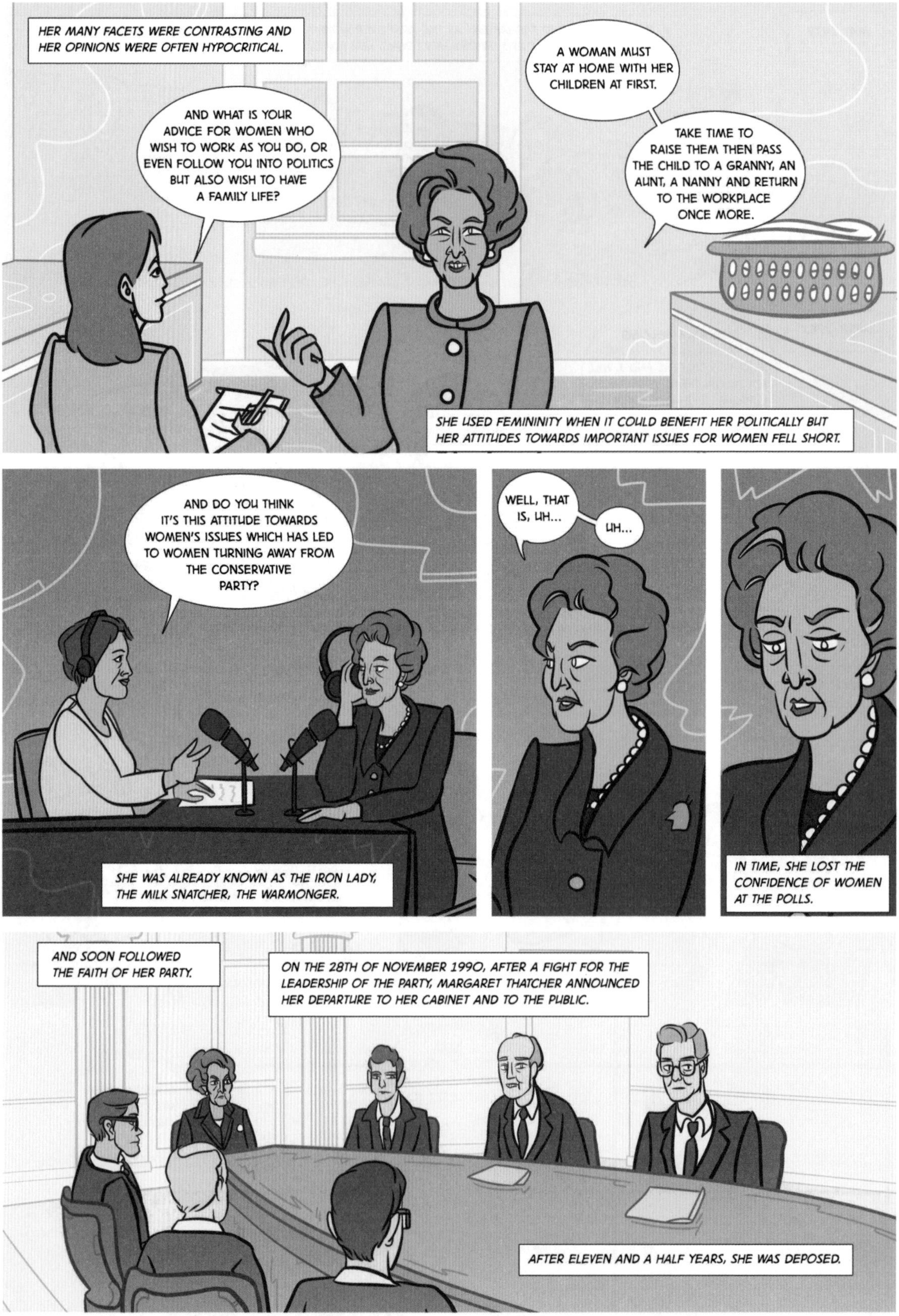
HER MANY FACETS WERE CONTRASTING AND HER OPINIONS WERE OFTEN HYPOCRITICAL.
AND WHAT IS YOUR ADVICE FOR WOMEN WHO WISH TO WORK AS YOU DO, OR EVEN FOLLOW YOU INTO POLITICS BUT ALSO WISH TO HAVE A FAMILY LIFE?
A WOMAN MUST STAY AT HOME WITH HER CHILDREN AT FIRST.
TAKE TIME TO RAISE THEM THEN PASS THE CHILD TO A GRANNY, AN AUNT, A NANNY AND RETURN TO THE WORKPLACE ONCE MORE.
SHE USED FEMININITY WHEN IT COULD BENEFIT HER POLITICALLY BUT HER ATTITUDES TOWARDS IMPORTANT ISSUES FOR WOMEN FELL SHORT.
AND DO YOU THINK IT'S THIS ATTITUDE TOWARDS WOMEN'S ISSUES WHICH HAS LED TO WOMEN TURNING AWAY FROM THE CONSERVATIVE PARTY?
SHE WAS ALREADY KNOWN AS THE IRON LADY, THE MILK SNATCHER, THE WARMONGER.
WELL, THAT IS, UH...
UH...
IN TIME, SHE LOST THE CONFIDENCE OF WOMEN AT THE POLLS.
AND SOON FOLLOWED THE FAITH OF HER PARTY.
ON THE 28TH OF NOVEMBER 1990, AFTER A FIGHT FOR THE LEADERSHIP OF THE PARTY, MARGARET THATCHER ANNOUNCED HER DEPARTURE TO HER CABINET AND TO THE PUBLIC.
AFTER ELEVEN AND A HALF YEARS, SHE WAS DEPOSED.

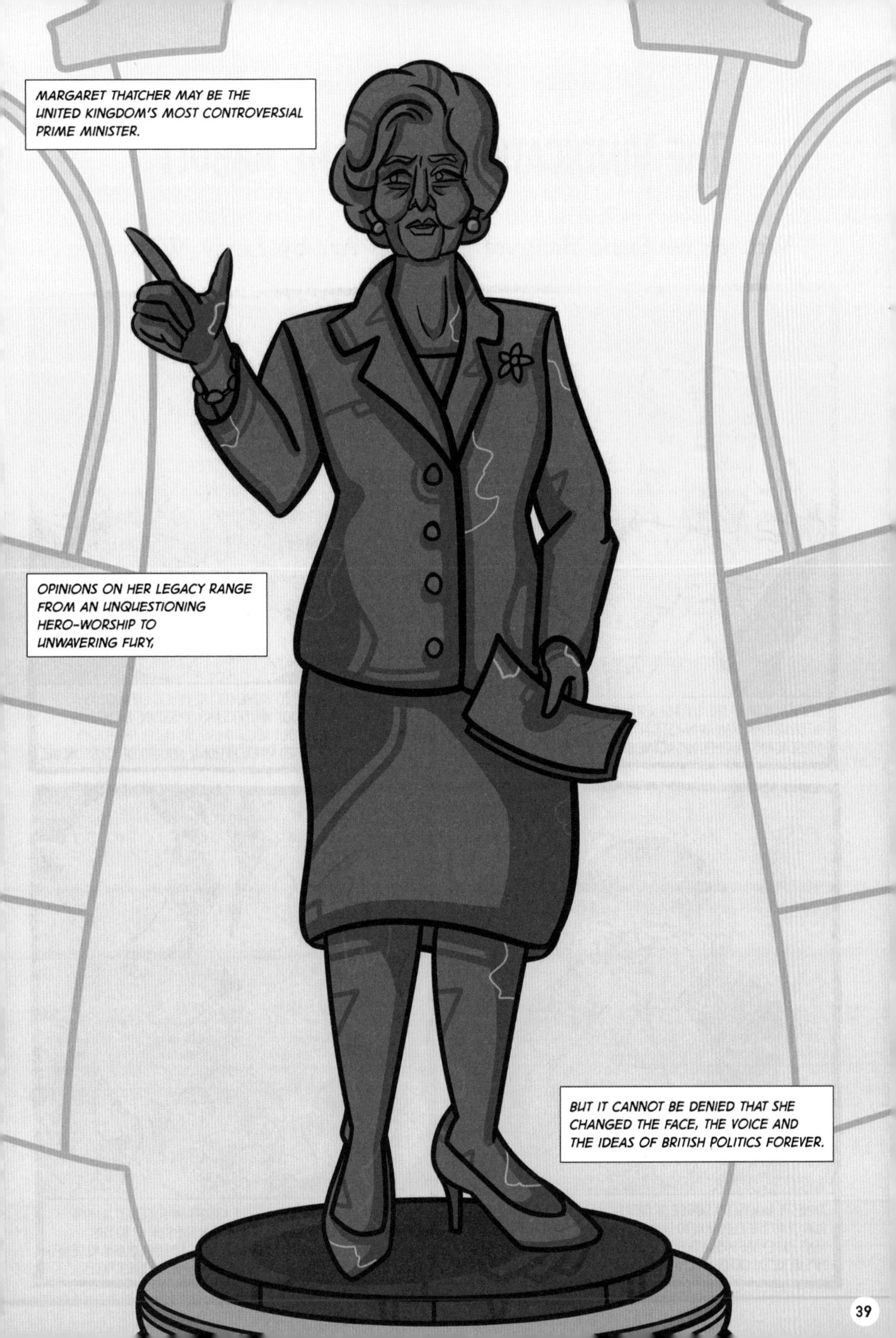
MARGARET THATCHER MAY BE THE UNITED KINGDOM'S MOST CONTROVERSIAL PRIME MINISTER.
OPINIONS ON HER LEGACY RANGE FROM AN UNQUESTIONING HERO-WORSHIP TO UNWAVERING FURY,
BUT IT CANNOT BE DENIED THAT SHE CHANGED THE FACE, THE VOICE AND THE IDEAS OF BRITISH POLITICS FOREVER.

THE VINDICATION OF DIANE ABBOTT

Written by Siana Bangura

Art by Letty Wilson

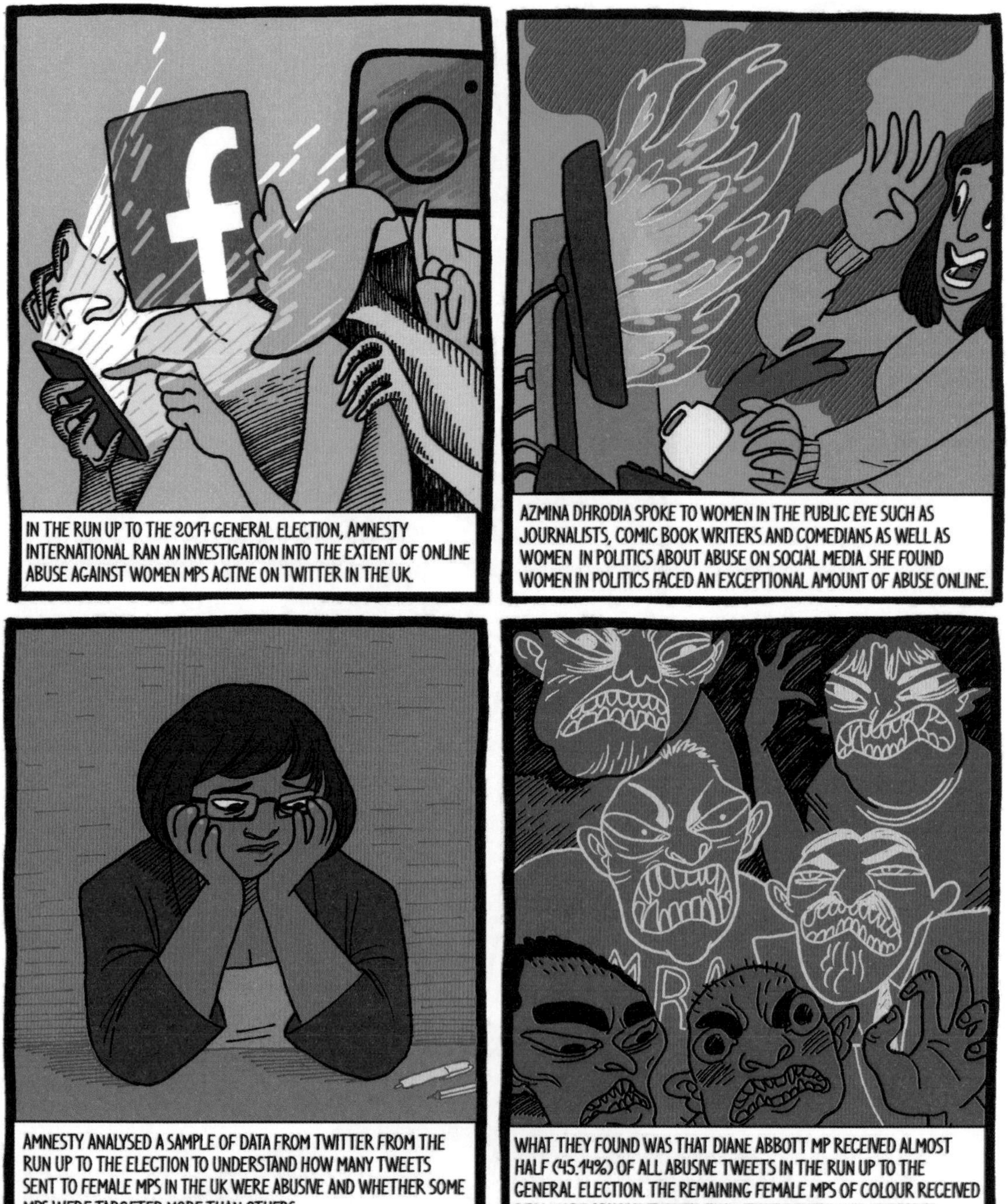
IN THE RUN UP TO THE 2017 GENERAL ELECTION, AMNESTY INTERNATIONAL RAN AN INVESTIGATION INTO THE EXTENT OF ONLINE ABUSE AGAINST WOMEN MPS ACTIVE ON TWITTER IN THE UK.
AZMINA DHRODIA SPOKE TO WOMEN IN THE PUBLIC EYE SUCH AS JOURNALISTS, COMIC BOOK WRITERS AND COMEDIANS AS WELL AS WOMEN IN POLITICS ABOUT ABUSE ON SOCIAL MEDIA. SHE FOUND WOMEN IN POLITICS FACED AN EXCEPTIONAL AMOUNT OF ABUSE ONLINE.
AMNESTY ANALYSED A SAMPLE OF DATA FROM TWITTER FROM THE RUN UP TO THE ELECTION TO UNDERSTAND HOW MANY TWEETS SENT TO FEMALE MPS IN THE UK WERE ABUSIVE AND WHETHER SOME MPS WERE TARGETED MORE THAN OTHERS.
WHAT THEY FOUND WAS THAT DIANE ABBOTT MP RECEIVED ALMOST HALF (45.14%) OF ALL ABUSIVE TWEETS IN THE RUN UP TO THE GENERAL ELECTION. THE REMAINING FEMALE MPS OF COLOUR RECEIVED 35% MORE ABUSIVE TWEETS THAN THEIR WHITE COUNTERPARTS.

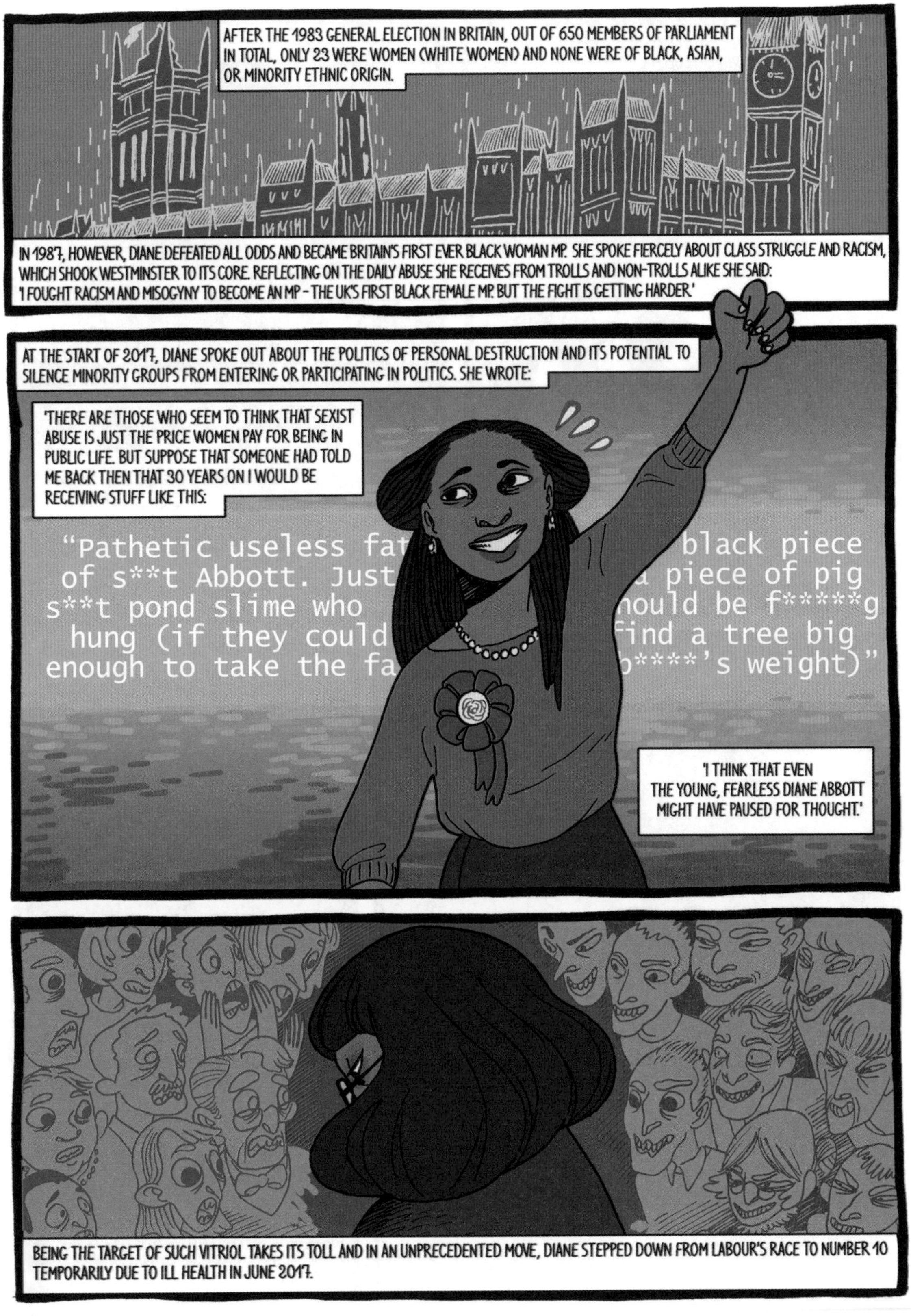
AFTER THE 1983 GENERAL ELECTION IN BRITAIN, OUT OF 650 MEMBERS OF PARLIAMENT IN TOTAL, ONLY 23 WERE WOMEN (WHITE WOMEN) AND NONE WERE OF BLACK, ASIAN, OR MINORITY ETHNIC ORIGIN.
IN 1987, HOWEVER, DIANE DEFEATED ALL ODDS AND BECAME BRITAIN'S FIRST EVER BLACK WOMAN MP. SHE SPOKE FIERCELY ABOUT CLASS STRUGGLE AND RACISM, WHICH SHOOK WESTMINSTER TO ITS CORE. REFLECTING ON THE DAILY ABUSE SHE RECEIVES FROM TROLLS AND NON-TROLLS ALIKE SHE SAID: 'I FOUGHT RACISM AND MISOGYNY TO BECOME AN MP – THE UK'S FIRST BLACK FEMALE MP. BUT THE FIGHT IS GETTING HARDER.'
AT THE START OF 2017, DIANE SPOKE OUT ABOUT THE POLITICS OF PERSONAL DESTRUCTION AND ITS POTENTIAL TO SILENCE MINORITY GROUPS FROM ENTERING OR PARTICIPATING IN POLITICS. SHE WROTE:
'THERE ARE THOSE WHO SEEM TO THINK THAT SEXIST ABUSE IS JUST THE PRICE WOMEN PAY FOR BEING IN PUBLIC LIFE. BUT SUPPOSE THAT SOMEONE HAD TOLD ME BACK THEN THAT 30 YEARS ON I WOULD BE RECEIVING STUFF LIKE THIS:
"Pathetic useless fat black piece
of s**t Abbott. Just piece of pig
s**t pond slime who hould be f*****g
hung (if they could find a tree big
enough to take the fa b****'s weight)"
'I THINK THAT EVEN THE YOUNG, FEARLESS DIANE ABBOTT MIGHT HAVE PAUSED FOR THOUGHT.'
BEING THE TARGET OF SUCH VITRIOL TAKES ITS TOLL AND IN AN UNPRECEDENTED MOVE, DIANE STEPPED DOWN FROM LABOUR'S RACE TO NUMBER 10 TEMPORARILY DUE TO ILL HEALTH IN JUNE 2017.

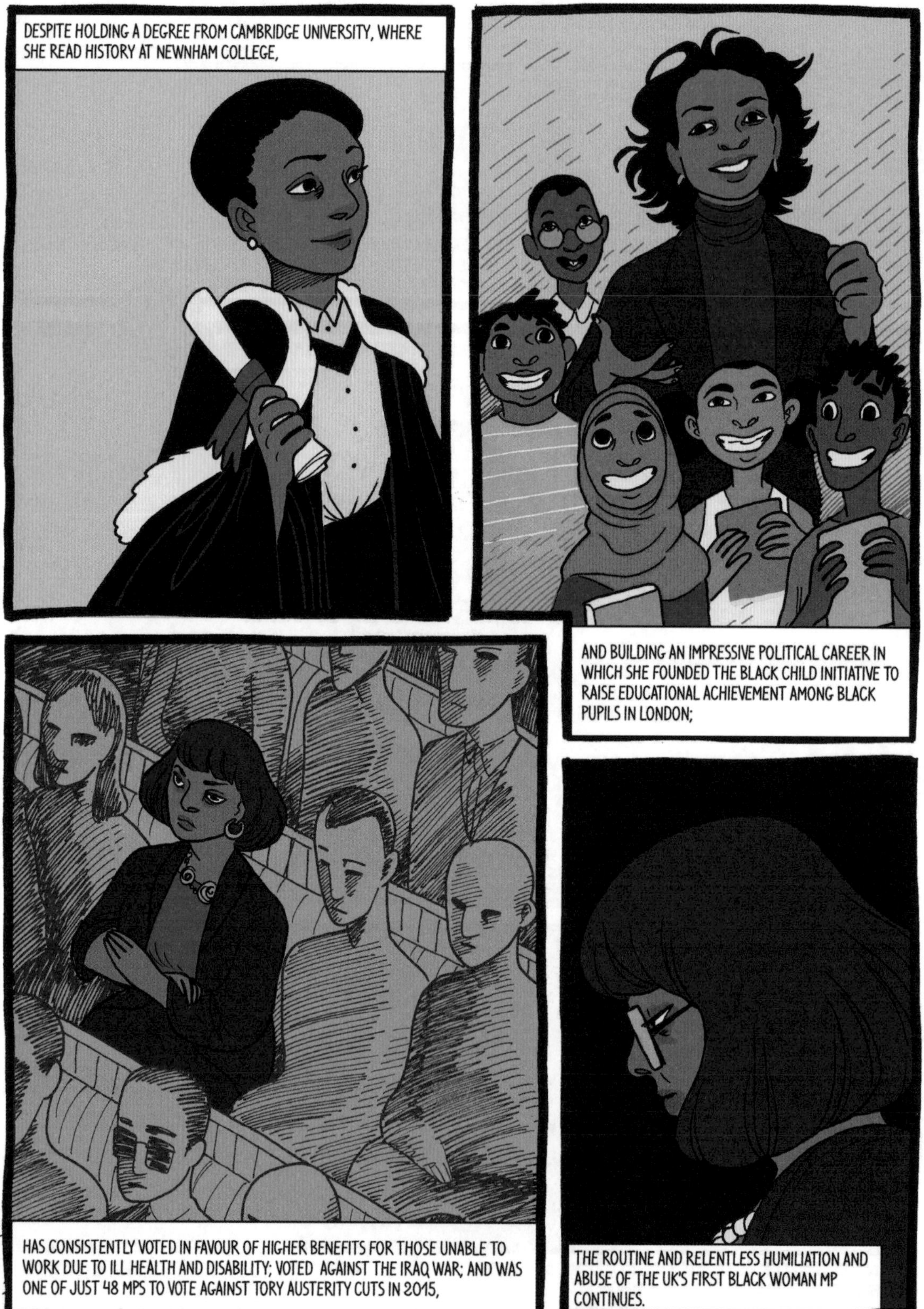
DESPITE HOLDING A DEGREE FROM CAMBRIDGE UNIVERSITY, WHERE SHE READ HISTORY AT NEWNHAM COLLEGE,
AND BUILDING AN IMPRESSIVE POLITICAL CAREER IN WHICH SHE FOUNDED THE BLACK CHILD INITIATIVE TO RAISE EDUCATIONAL ACHIEVEMENT AMONG BLACK PUPILS IN LONDON;
HAS CONSISTENTLY VOTED IN FAVOUR OF HIGHER BENEFITS FOR THOSE UNABLE TO WORK DUE TO ILL HEALTH AND DISABILITY; VOTED AGAINST THE IRAQ WAR; AND WAS ONE OF JUST 48 MPS TO VOTE AGAINST TORY AUSTERITY CUTS IN 2015,
THE ROUTINE AND RELENTLESS HUMILIATION AND ABUSE OF THE UK'S FIRST BLACK WOMAN MP CONTINUES.

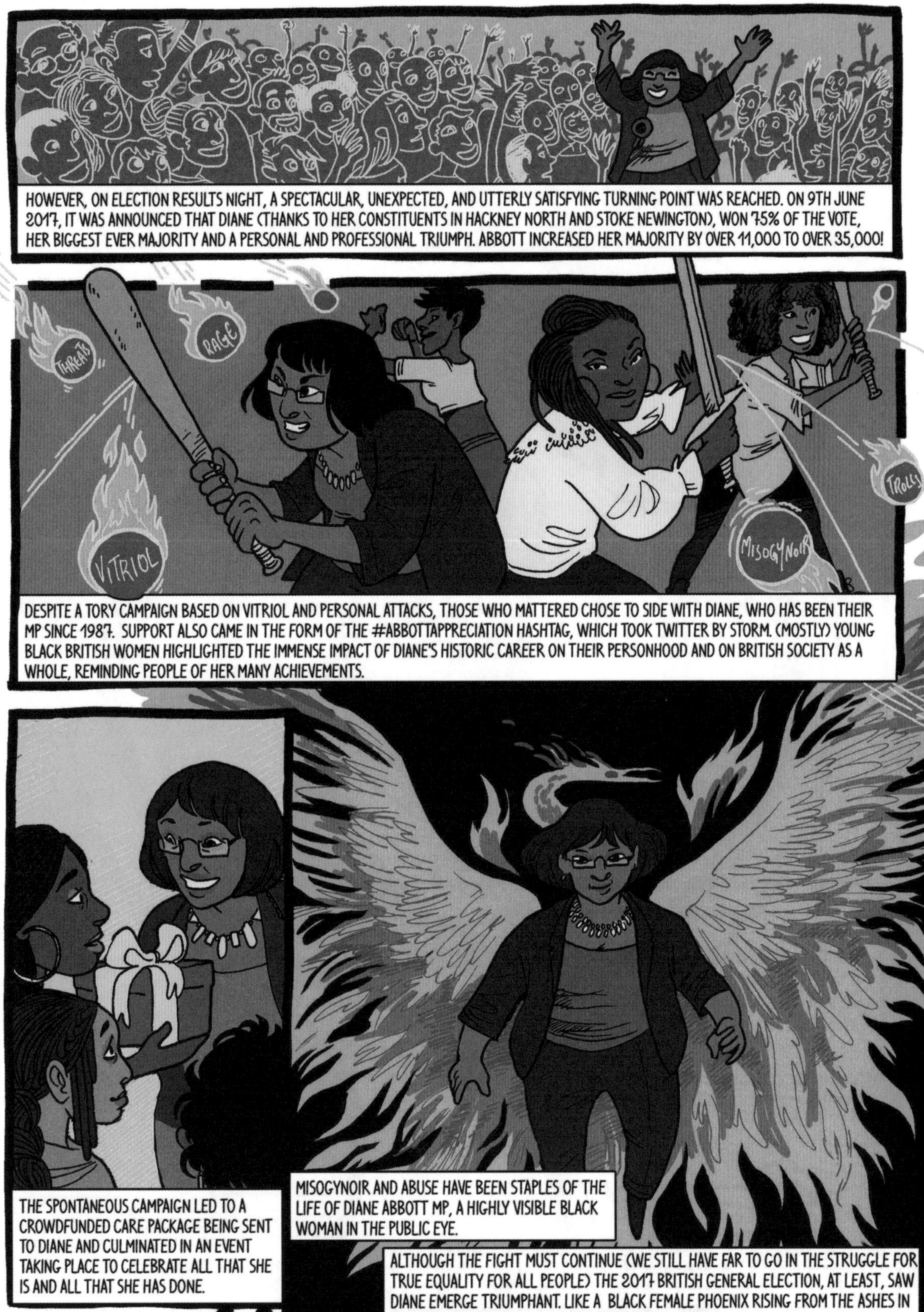
HOWEVER, ON ELECTION RESULTS NIGHT, A SPECTACULAR, UNEXPECTED, AND UTTERLY SATISFYING TURNING POINT WAS REACHED. ON 9TH JUNE 2017, IT WAS ANNOUNCED THAT DIANE (THANKS TO HER CONSTITUENTS IN HACKNEY NORTH AND STOKE NEWINGTON), WON 75% OF THE VOTE, HER BIGGEST EVER MAJORITY AND A PERSONAL AND PROFESSIONAL TRIUMPH. ABBOTT INCREASED HER MAJORITY BY OVER 11,000 TO OVER 35,000!
THREATS
RAGE
VITRIOL
TROLLS
MISOGYNOIR
DESPITE A TORY CAMPAIGN BASED ON VITRIOL AND PERSONAL ATTACKS, THOSE WHO MATTERED CHOSE TO SIDE WITH DIANE, WHO HAS BEEN THEIR MP SINCE 1987. SUPPORT ALSO CAME IN THE FORM OF THE #ABBOTTAPPRECIATION HASHTAG, WHICH TOOK TWITTER BY STORM. (MOSTLY) YOUNG BLACK BRITISH WOMEN HIGHLIGHTED THE IMMENSE IMPACT OF DIANE'S HISTORIC CAREER ON THEIR PERSONHOOD AND ON BRITISH SOCIETY AS A WHOLE, REMINDING PEOPLE OF HER MANY ACHIEVEMENTS.
THE SPONTANEOUS CAMPAIGN LED TO A CROWDFUNDED CARE PACKAGE BEING SENT TO DIANE AND CULMINATED IN AN EVENT TAKING PLACE TO CELEBRATE ALL THAT SHE IS AND ALL THAT SHE HAS DONE.
MISOGYNOIR AND ABUSE HAVE BEEN STAPLES OF THE LIFE OF DIANE ABBOTT MP, A HIGHLY VISIBLE BLACK WOMAN IN THE PUBLIC EYE.
ALTHOUGH THE FIGHT MUST CONTINUE (WE STILL HAVE FAR TO GO IN THE STRUGGLE FOR TRUE EQUALITY FOR ALL PEOPLE) THE 2017 BRITISH GENERAL ELECTION, AT LEAST, SAW DIANE EMERGE TRIUMPHANT. LIKE A BLACK FEMALE PHOENIX RISING FROM THE ASHES IN THE FACE OF SCRUTINY, SHE WAS VINDICATED - FINALLY.

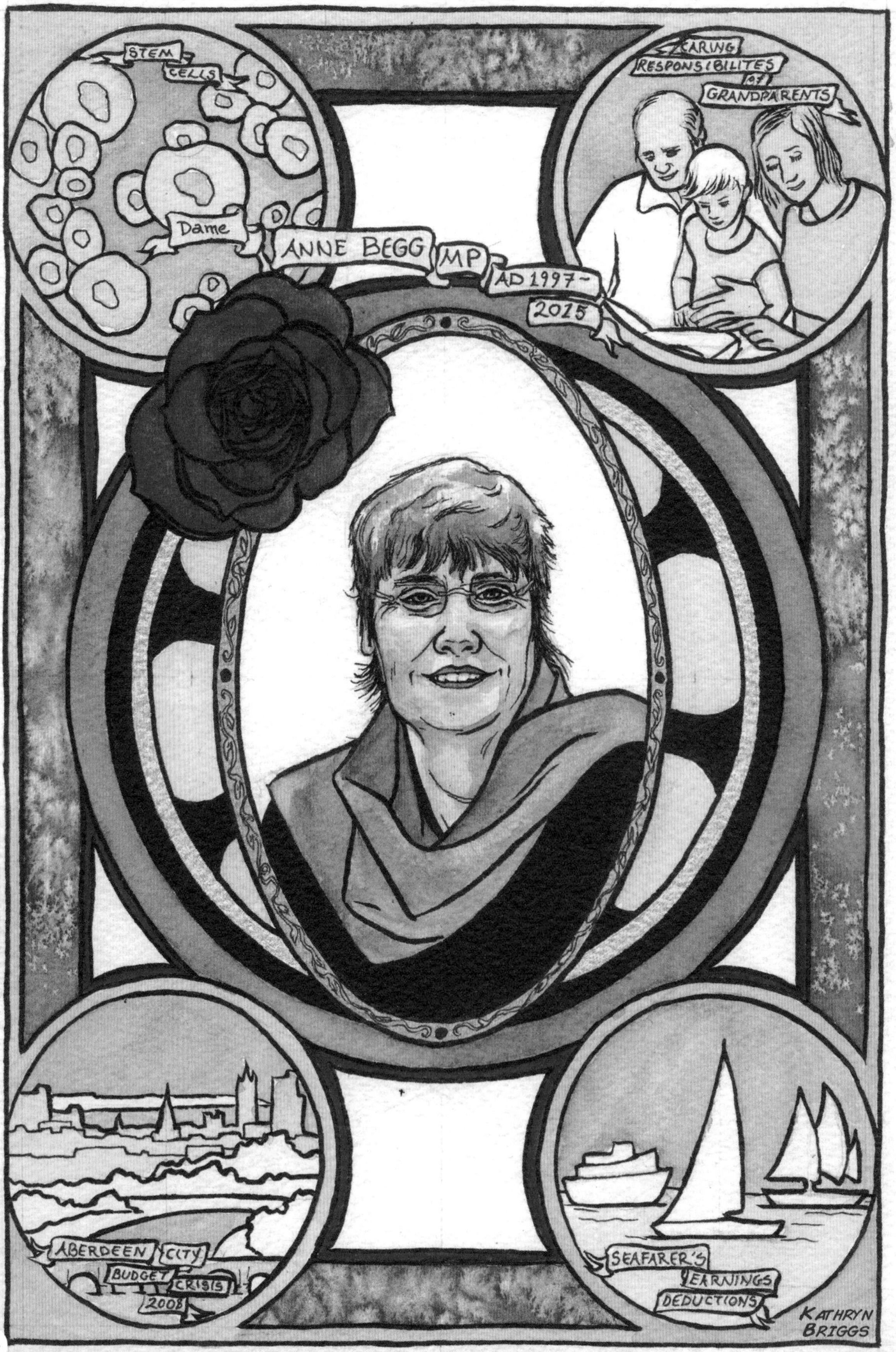
STEM CELLS
CARING RESPONSIBILITES of GRANDPARENTS
Dame ANNE BEGG MP AD 1997 - 2015
ABERDEEN CITY BUDGET CRISIS 2008
SEAFARER'S EARNINGS DEDUCTIONS
KATHRYN BRIGGS

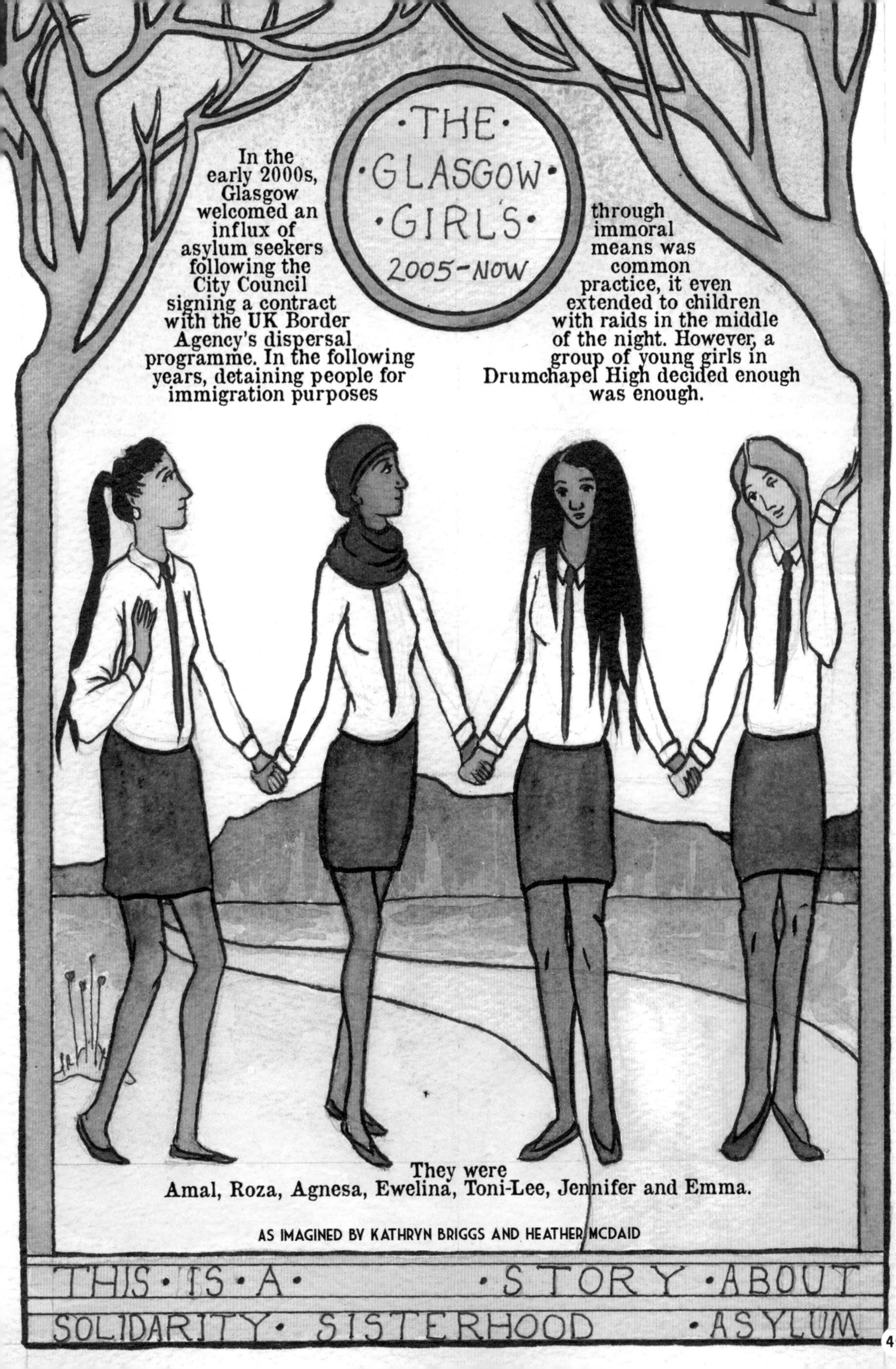

·THE· ·GLASGOW· ·GIRLS· 2005–NOW
In the early 2000s, Glasgow welcomed an influx of asylum seekers following the City Council signing a contract with the UK Border Agency's dispersal programme. In the following years, detaining people for immigration purposes
through immoral means was common practice, it even extended to children with raids in the middle of the night. However, a group of young girls in Drumchapel High decided enough was enough.
They were Amal, Roza, Agnesa, Ewelina, Toni-Lee, Jennifer and Emma.
AS IMAGINED BY KATHRYN BRIGGS AND HEATHER MCDAID
THIS·IS·A· ·STORY·ABOUT
SOLIDARITY· SISTERHOOD ·ASYLUM

Schoolgirl Agnesa Murselaj, her parents Sadush and Tade, and siblings Gentian and Leonard, faced deportation to Kosovo, and were taken to and held in Yarl's Wood detention centre.

The Drumchapel High collective refused to let their friend and fellow student be another statistic, rallying behind her family to launch a campaign and petition that changed everything.

The Murselaj family were rightfully allowed to stay, for the time being. It in fact took until 2008 for them to receive permanent leave to remain, but the Glasgow Girls continued - they did not rest.

The girls rose their voices, spoke out with concern as more children at their school faced similar fates: the dawn raids, detainment and deportation. It grew beyond Drumchapel High.

By September 2005, their campaigning to support asylum seekers had gained national attention. Dozens of MSPs signed a parliamentary motion praising the pupil's actions; they gained cross-party support.

And still, their voices grew louder, speaking from experience, from seeing their friends lives being torn apart. Even with the admiration of Scottish Parliament and press, forward they moved, challenging Jack McConnell, the then First Minister, on the treatment of asylum seekers. No more empty promises.

They were lavished in praise. Emma said: "I felt like people were congratulating us so much yesterday that they weren't actually listening to our questions. I think they should start congratulating us when the situation has changed, not yet."*

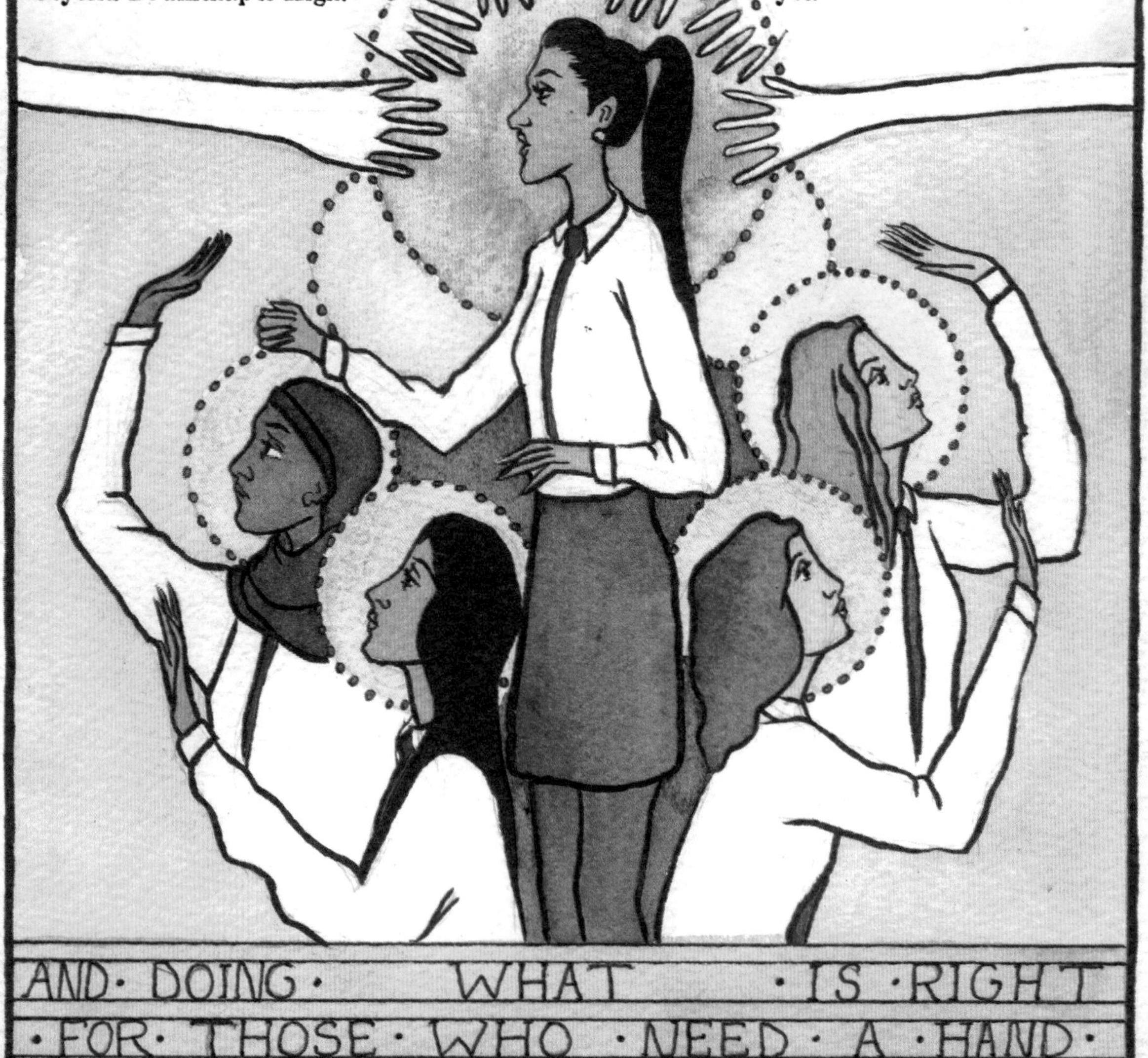
AND · DOING · WHAT · IS · RIGHT
· FOR · THOSE · WHO · NEED · A · HAND ·
EVEN · WHEN · YOU · NEED · ONE · TOO

*SOURCE: The Herald, 'Glasgow Girls who shamed our first minister into asylum U-turn Executive forced to take action over policy on immigration', 24 Sep 2005

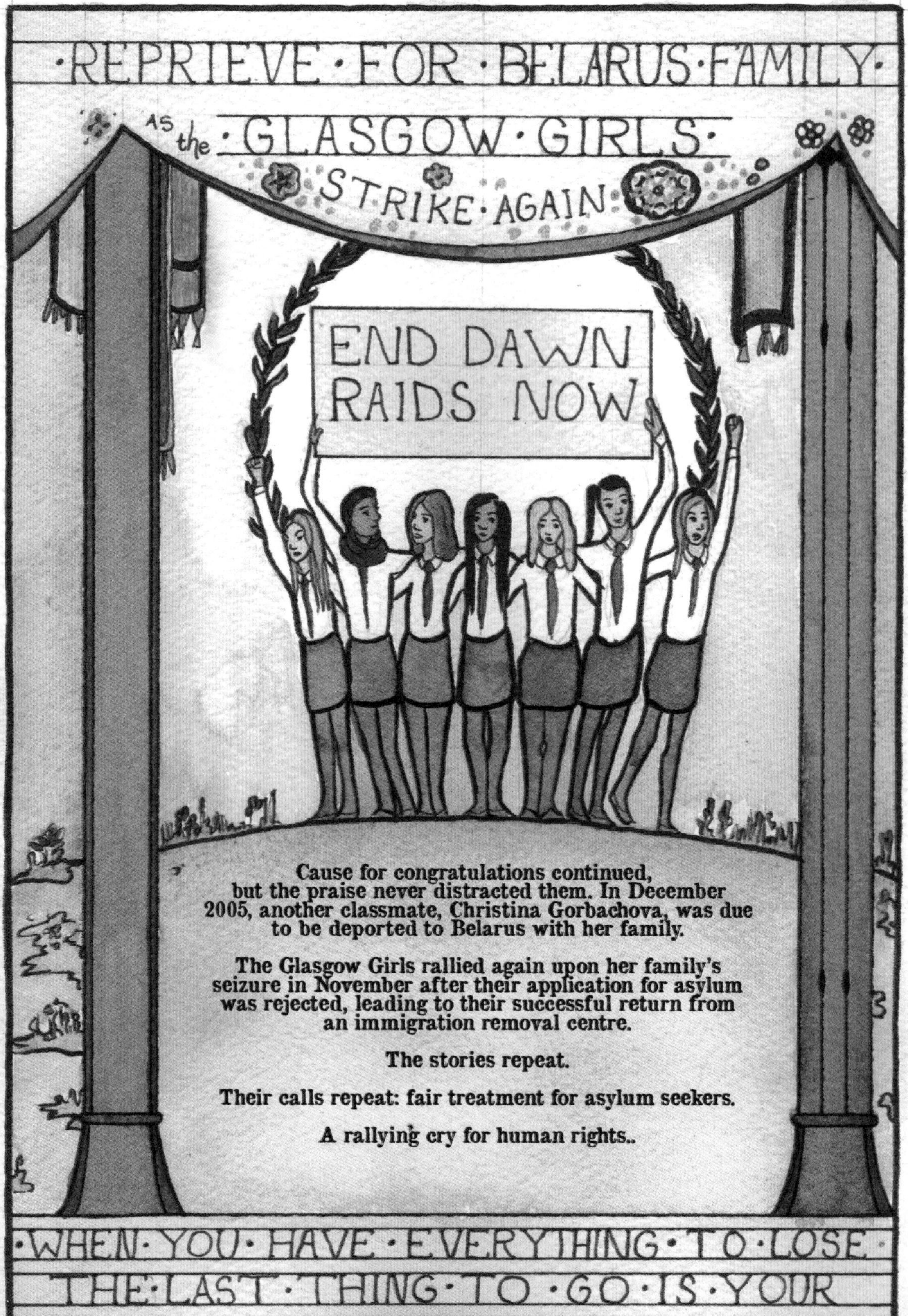
·REPRIEVE·FOR·BELARUS·FAMILY·
AS the ·GLASGOW·GIRLS·
STRIKE·AGAIN
END DAWN RAIDS NOW
Cause for congratulations continued, but the praise never distracted them. In December 2005, another classmate, Christina Gorbachova, was due to be deported to Belarus with her family.
The Glasgow Girls rallied again upon her family's seizure in November after their application for asylum was rejected, leading to their successful return from an immigration removal centre.
The stories repeat.
Their calls repeat: fair treatment for asylum seekers.
A rallying cry for human rights..
·WHEN·YOU·HAVE·EVERYTHING·TO·LOSE
THE·LAST·THING·TO·GO·IS·YOUR
·COMPASSION·

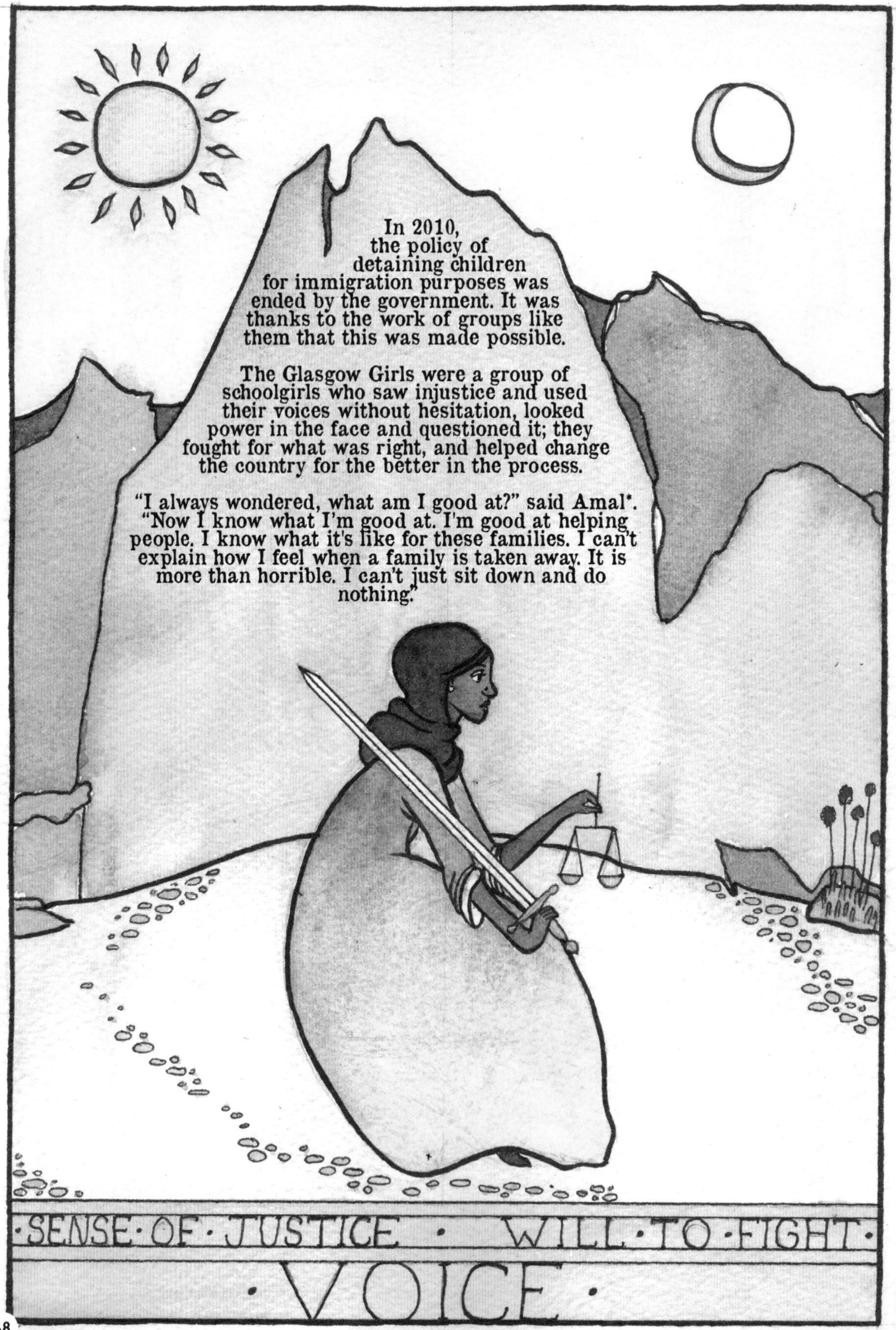
In 2010, the policy of detaining children for immigration purposes was ended by the government. It was thanks to the work of groups like them that this was made possible.
The Glasgow Girls were a group of schoolgirls who saw injustice and used their voices without hesitation, looked power in the face and questioned it; they fought for what was right, and helped change the country for the better in the process.
"I always wondered, what am I good at?" said Amal*. "Now I know what I'm good at. I'm good at helping people. I know what it's like for these families. I can't explain how I feel when a family is taken away. It is more than horrible. I can't just sit down and do nothing."
·SENSE·OF·JUSTICE · WILL·TO·FIGHT·
·VOICE·

*SOURCE: The Herald, '15-Year-Old Amal Azzudin formed the Glasgow Girls..', 11 Dec 2005

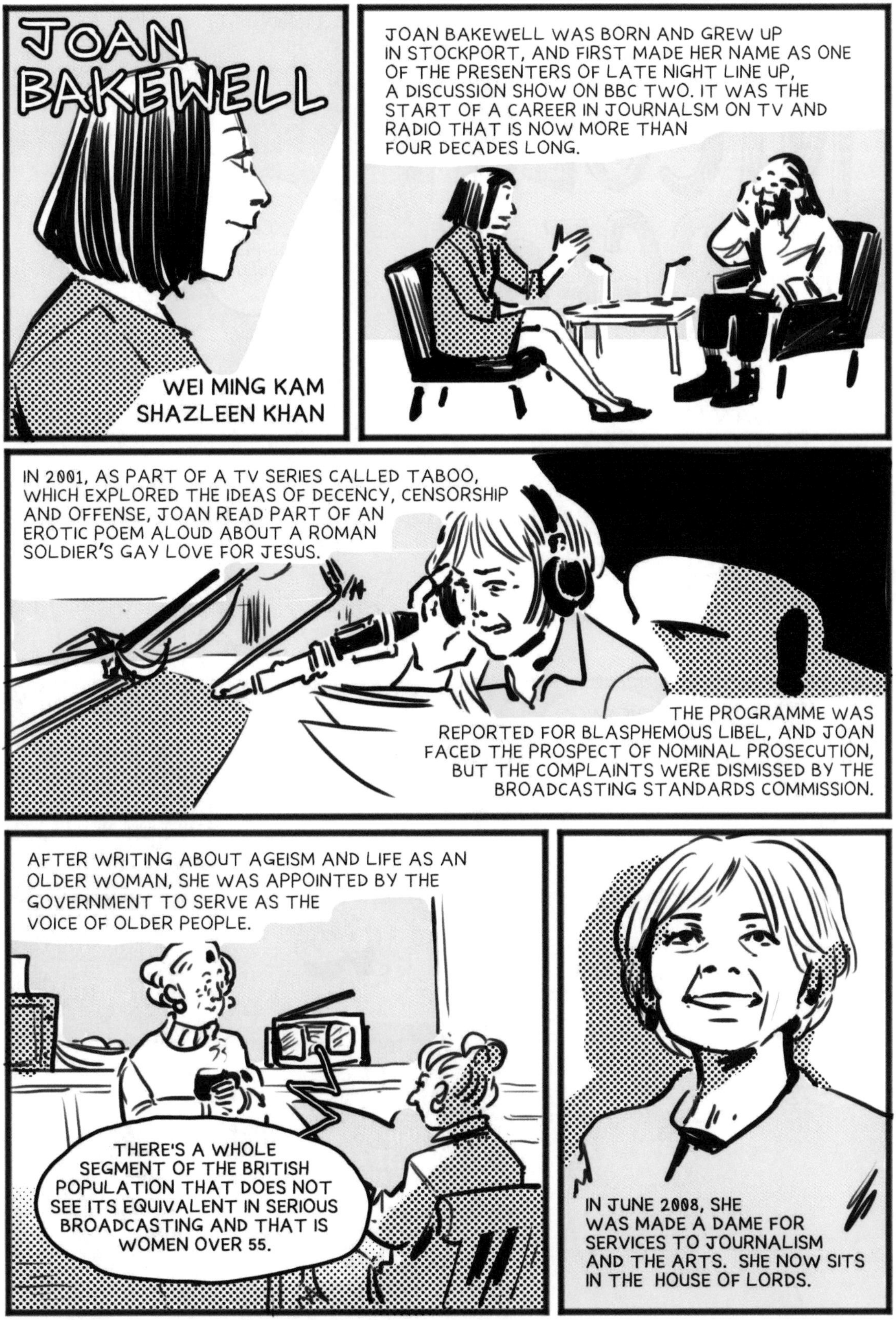
JOAN BAKEWELL
WEI MING KAM
SHAZLEEN KHAN
JOAN BAKEWELL WAS BORN AND GREW UP IN STOCKPORT, AND FIRST MADE HER NAME AS ONE OF THE PRESENTERS OF LATE NIGHT LINE UP, A DISCUSSION SHOW ON BBC TWO. IT WAS THE START OF A CAREER IN JOURNALSM ON TV AND RADIO THAT IS NOW MORE THAN FOUR DECADES LONG.
IN 2001, AS PART OF A TV SERIES CALLED TABOO, WHICH EXPLORED THE IDEAS OF DECENCY, CENSORSHIP AND OFFENSE, JOAN READ PART OF AN EROTIC POEM ALOUD ABOUT A ROMAN SOLDIER'S GAY LOVE FOR JESUS.
THE PROGRAMME WAS REPORTED FOR BLASPHEMOUS LIBEL, AND JOAN FACED THE PROSPECT OF NOMINAL PROSECUTION, BUT THE COMPLAINTS WERE DISMISSED BY THE BROADCASTING STANDARDS COMMISSION.
AFTER WRITING ABOUT AGEISM AND LIFE AS AN OLDER WOMAN, SHE WAS APPOINTED BY THE GOVERNMENT TO SERVE AS THE VOICE OF OLDER PEOPLE.
THERE'S A WHOLE SEGMENT OF THE BRITISH POPULATION THAT DOES NOT SEE ITS EQUIVALENT IN SERIOUS BROADCASTING AND THAT IS WOMEN OVER 55.
IN JUNE 2008, SHE WAS MADE A DAME FOR SERVICES TO JOURNALISM AND THE ARTS. SHE NOW SITS IN THE HOUSE OF LORDS.

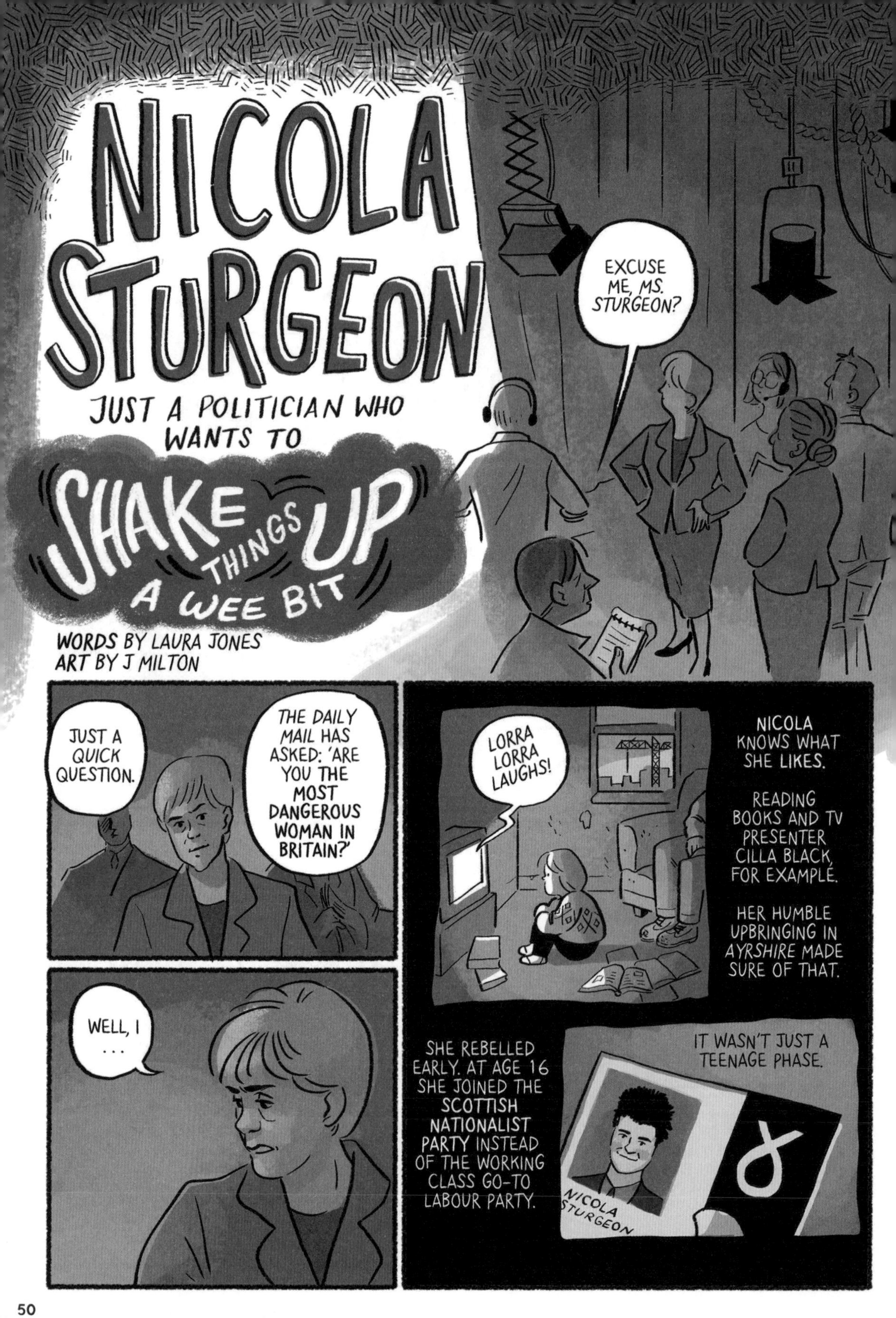
NICOLA STURGEON
JUST A POLITICIAN WHO WANTS TO
SHAKE THINGS UP A WEE BIT
WORDS BY LAURA JONES
ART BY J MILTON
EXCUSE ME, MS. STURGEON?
JUST A QUICK QUESTION.
THE DAILY MAIL HAS ASKED: 'ARE YOU THE MOST DANGEROUS WOMAN IN BRITAIN?'
WELL, I . . .
LORRA LORRA LAUGHS!
NICOLA KNOWS WHAT SHE LIKES.
READING BOOKS AND TV PRESENTER CILLA BLACK, FOR EXAMPLE.
HER HUMBLE UPBRINGING IN AYRSHIRE MADE SURE OF THAT.
SHE REBELLED EARLY. AT AGE 16 SHE JOINED THE SCOTTISH NATIONALIST PARTY INSTEAD OF THE WORKING CLASS GO-TO LABOUR PARTY.
IT WASN'T JUST A TEENAGE PHASE.
NICOLA STURGEON

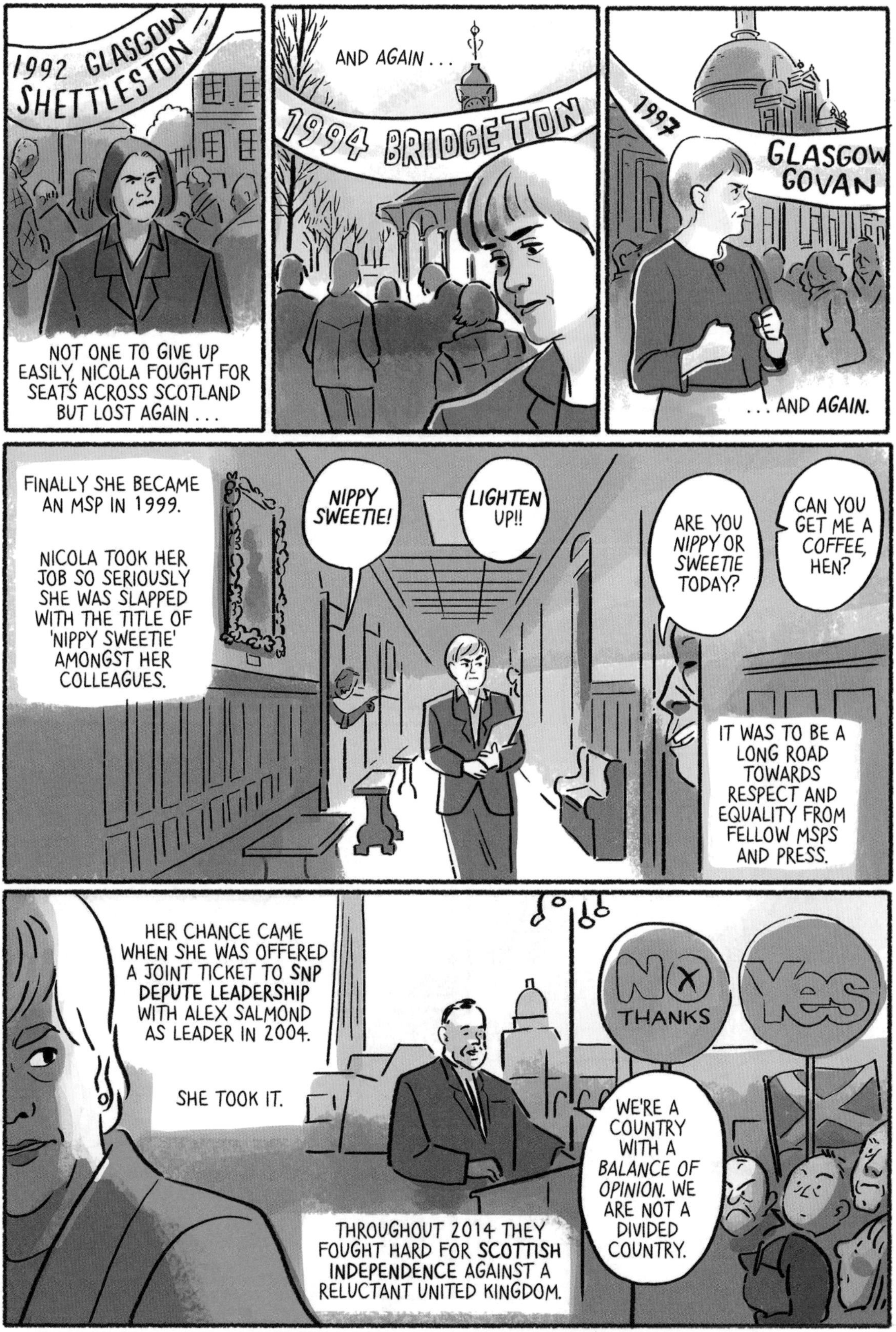
1992 GLASGOW SHETTLESTON
NOT ONE TO GIVE UP EASILY, NICOLA FOUGHT FOR SEATS ACROSS SCOTLAND BUT LOST AGAIN . . .
AND AGAIN . . .
1994 BRIDGETON
1997 GLASGOW GOVAN
. . . AND AGAIN.
FINALLY SHE BECAME AN MSP IN 1999.
NICOLA TOOK HER JOB SO SERIOUSLY SHE WAS SLAPPED WITH THE TITLE OF 'NIPPY SWEETIE' AMONGST HER COLLEAGUES.
NIPPY SWEETIE!
LIGHTEN UP!!
ARE YOU NIPPY OR SWEETIE TODAY?
CAN YOU GET ME A COFFEE, HEN?
IT WAS TO BE A LONG ROAD TOWARDS RESPECT AND EQUALITY FROM FELLOW MSPS AND PRESS.
HER CHANCE CAME WHEN SHE WAS OFFERED A JOINT TICKET TO SNP DEPUTE LEADERSHIP WITH ALEX SALMOND AS LEADER IN 2004.
SHE TOOK IT.
NO THANKS
Yes
WE'RE A COUNTRY WITH A BALANCE OF OPINION. WE ARE NOT A DIVIDED COUNTRY.
THROUGHOUT 2014 THEY FOUGHT HARD FOR SCOTTISH INDEPENDENCE AGAINST A RELUCTANT UNITED KINGDOM.

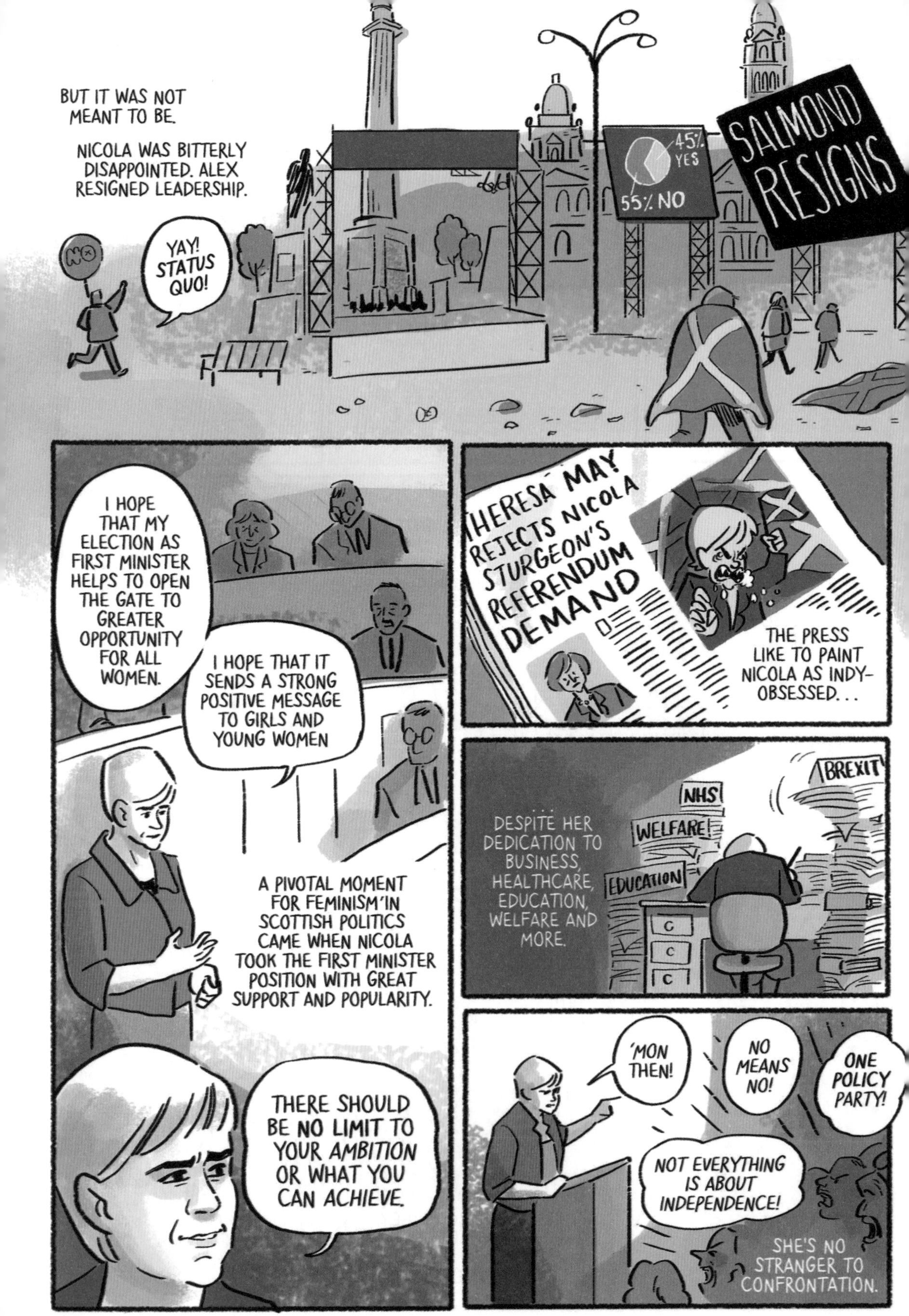
BUT IT WAS NOT MEANT TO BE.
NICOLA WAS BITTERLY DISAPPOINTED. ALEX RESIGNED LEADERSHIP.
SALMOND RESIGNS
45% YES
55% NO
NO
YAY! STATUS QUO!
I HOPE THAT MY ELECTION AS FIRST MINISTER HELPS TO OPEN THE GATE TO GREATER OPPORTUNITY FOR ALL WOMEN.
I HOPE THAT IT SENDS A STRONG POSITIVE MESSAGE TO GIRLS AND YOUNG WOMEN
A PIVOTAL MOMENT FOR FEMINISM IN SCOTTISH POLITICS CAME WHEN NICOLA TOOK THE FIRST MINISTER POSITION WITH GREAT SUPPORT AND POPULARITY.
THERE SHOULD BE NO LIMIT TO YOUR AMBITION OR WHAT YOU CAN ACHIEVE.
THERESA MAY REJECTS NICOLA STURGEON'S REFERENDUM DEMAND
THE PRESS LIKE TO PAINT NICOLA AS INDY-OBSESSED...
... DESPITE HER DEDICATION TO BUSINESS, HEALTHCARE, EDUCATION, WELFARE AND MORE.
BREXIT
NHS
WELFARE!
EDUCATION
'MON THEN!
NO MEANS NO!
ONE POLICY PARTY!
NOT EVERYTHING IS ABOUT INDEPENDENCE!
SHE'S NO STRANGER TO CONFRONTATION.

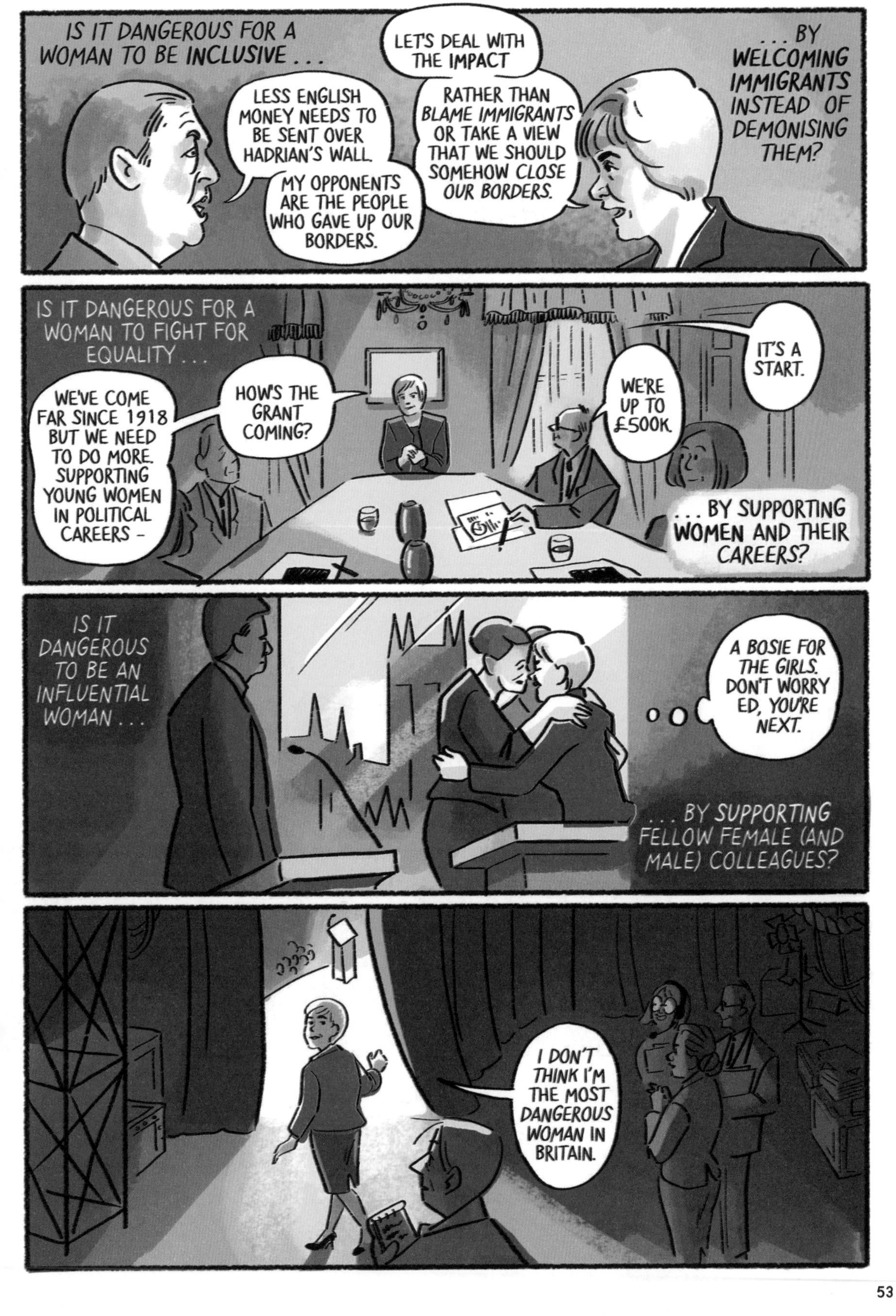
IS IT DANGEROUS FOR A WOMAN TO BE INCLUSIVE . . .
LESS ENGLISH MONEY NEEDS TO BE SENT OVER HADRIAN'S WALL.
MY OPPONENTS ARE THE PEOPLE WHO GAVE UP OUR BORDERS.
LET'S DEAL WITH THE IMPACT
RATHER THAN BLAME IMMIGRANTS OR TAKE A VIEW THAT WE SHOULD SOMEHOW CLOSE OUR BORDERS.
. . . BY WELCOMING IMMIGRANTS INSTEAD OF DEMONISING THEM?
IS IT DANGEROUS FOR A WOMAN TO FIGHT FOR EQUALITY . . .
WE'VE COME FAR SINCE 1918 BUT WE NEED TO DO MORE. SUPPORTING YOUNG WOMEN IN POLITICAL CAREERS –
HOW'S THE GRANT COMING?
WE'RE UP TO £500K.
IT'S A START.
. . . BY SUPPORTING WOMEN AND THEIR CAREERS?
IS IT DANGEROUS TO BE AN INFLUENTIAL WOMAN . . .
A BOSIE FOR THE GIRLS. DON'T WORRY ED, YOU'RE NEXT.
. . . BY SUPPORTING FELLOW FEMALE (AND MALE) COLLEAGUES?
I DON'T THINK I'M THE MOST DANGEROUS WOMAN IN BRITAIN.

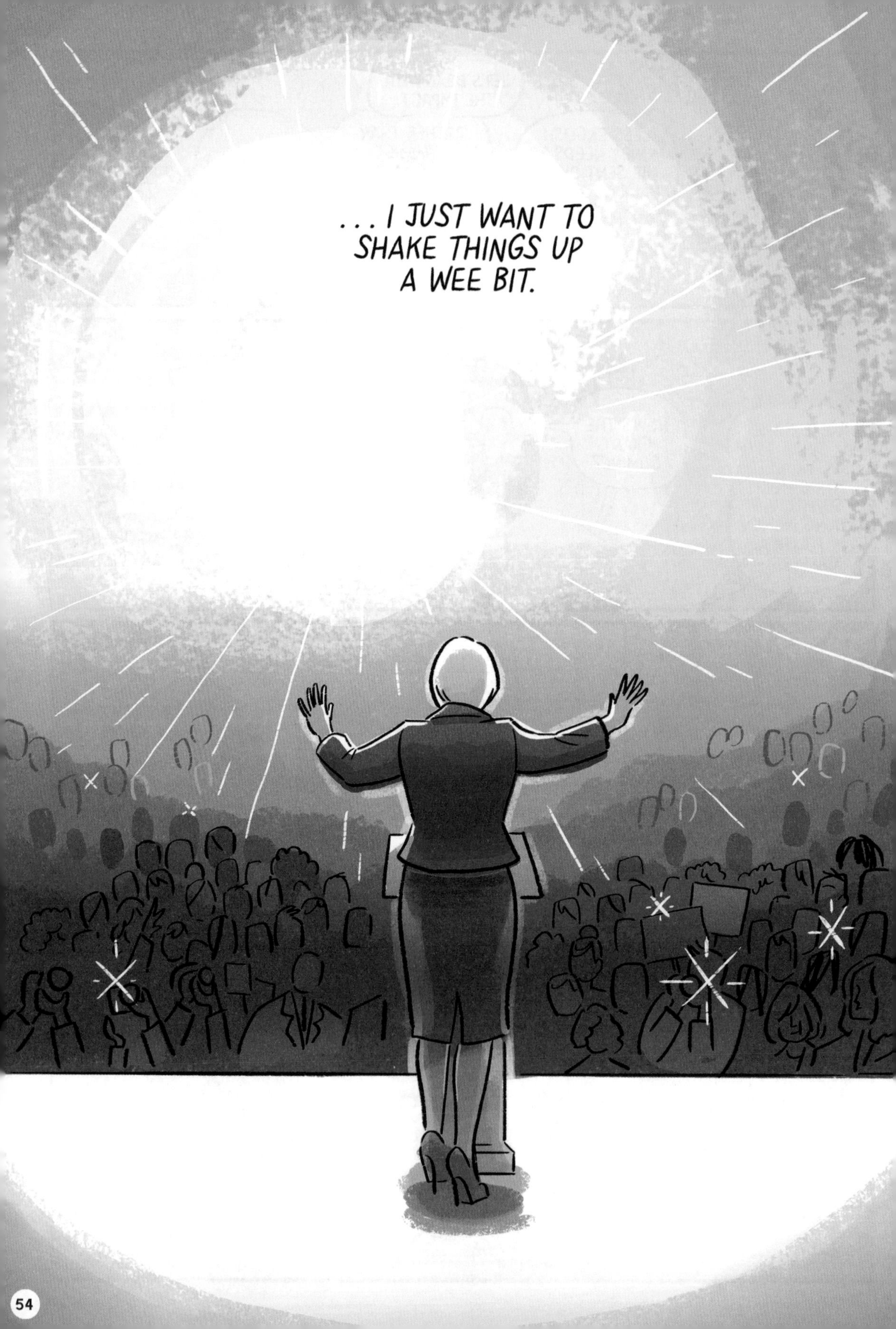
...I JUST WANT TO SHAKE THINGS UP A WEE BIT.

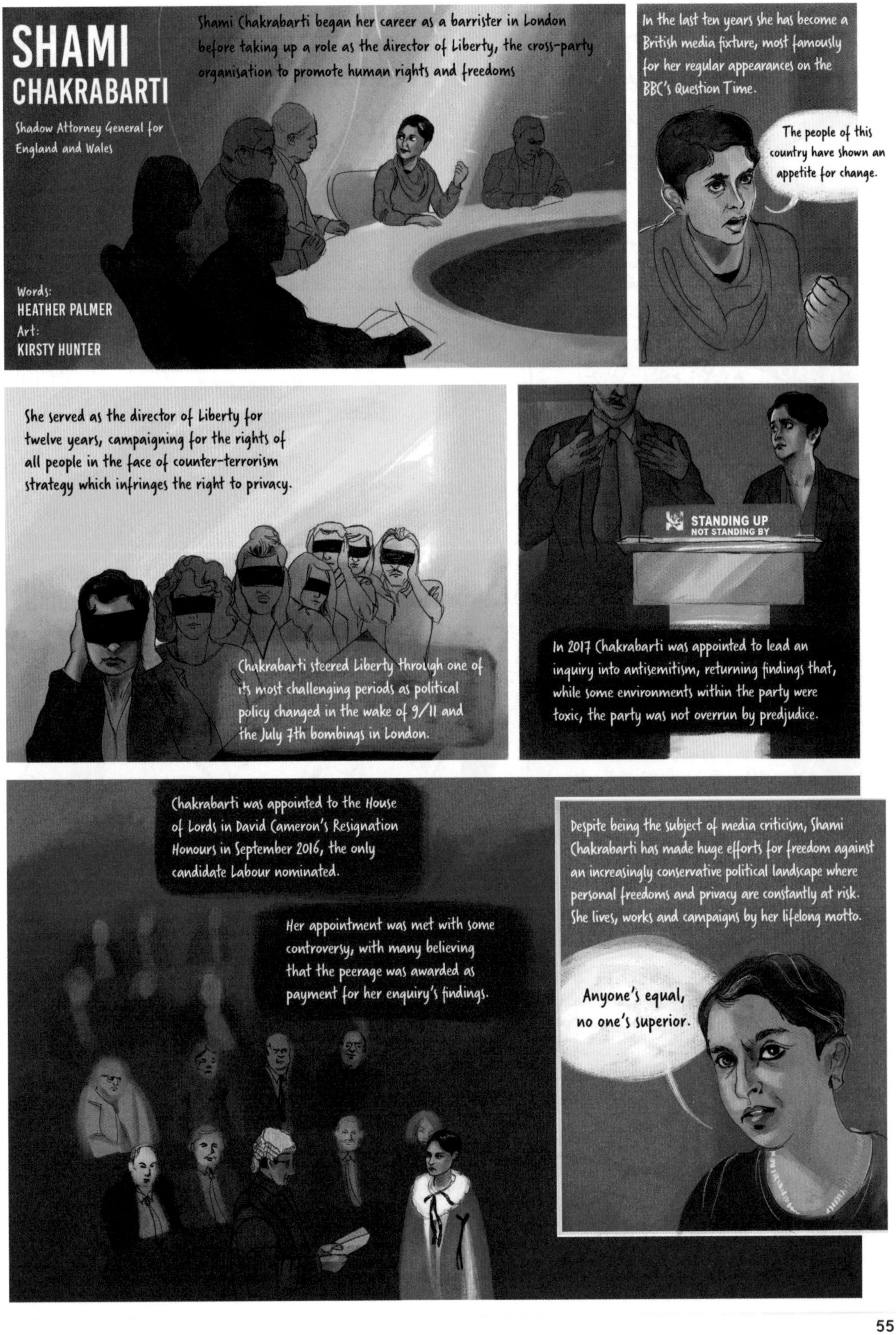
SHAMI
CHAKRABARTI
Shadow Attorney General for England and Wales
Words:
HEATHER PALMER
Art:
KIRSTY HUNTER
Shami Chakrabarti began her career as a barrister in London before taking up a role as the director of Liberty, the cross-party organisation to promote human rights and freedoms
In the last ten years she has become a British media fixture, most famously for her regular appearances on the BBC's Question Time.
The people of this country have shown an appetite for change.
She served as the director of Liberty for twelve years, campaigning for the rights of all people in the face of counter-terrorism strategy which infringes the right to privacy.
Chakrabarti steered Liberty through one of its most challenging periods as political policy changed in the wake of 9/11 and the July 7th bombings in London.
STANDING UP
NOT STANDING BY
In 2017 Chakrabarti was appointed to lead an inquiry into antisemitism, returning findings that, while some environments within the party were toxic, the party was not overrun by predjudice.
Chakrabarti was appointed to the House of Lords in David Cameron's Resignation Honours in September 2016, the only candidate Labour nominated.
Her appointment was met with some controversy, with many believing that the peerage was awarded as payment for her enquiry's findings.
Despite being the subject of media criticism, Shami Chakrabarti has made huge efforts for freedom against an increasingly conservative political landscape where personal freedoms and privacy are constantly at risk. She lives, works and campaigns by her lifelong motto.
Anyone's equal, no one's superior.

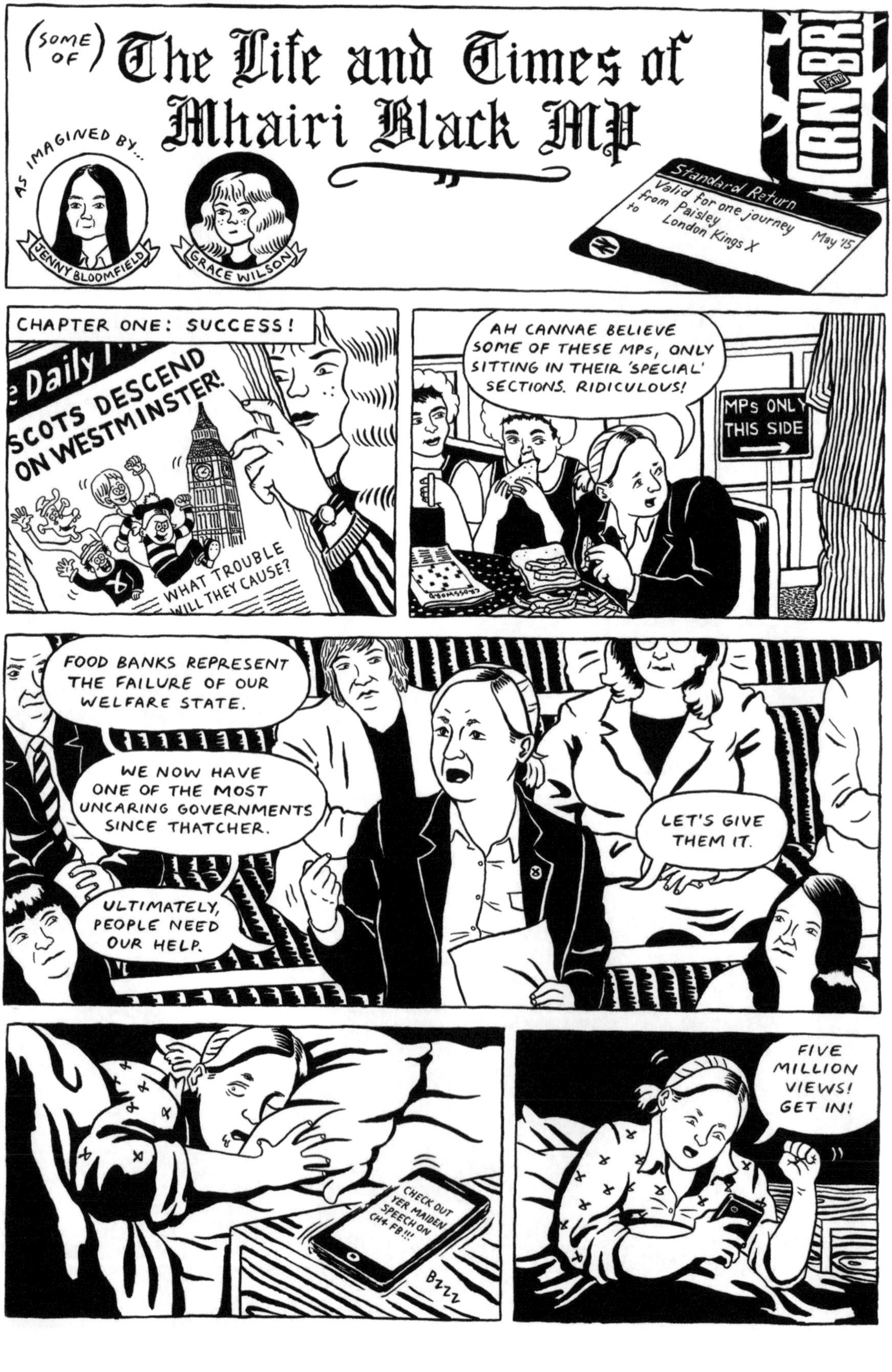
(SOME OF) The Life and Times of Mhairi Black MP
AS IMAGINED BY...
JENNY BLOOMFIELD
GRACE WILSON
IRN BRU
BARR
Standard Return
Valid for one journey from Paisley to London Kings X
May '15
CHAPTER ONE: SUCCESS!
SCOTS DESCEND ON WESTMINSTER!
WHAT TROUBLE WILL THEY CAUSE?
AH CANNAE BELIEVE SOME OF THESE MPs, ONLY SITTING IN THEIR 'SPECIAL' SECTIONS. RIDICULOUS!
MPs ONLY THIS SIDE
FOOD BANKS REPRESENT THE FAILURE OF OUR WELFARE STATE.
WE NOW HAVE ONE OF THE MOST UNCARING GOVERNMENTS SINCE THATCHER.
ULTIMATELY, PEOPLE NEED OUR HELP.
LET'S GIVE THEM IT.
CHECK OUT YER MAIDEN SPEECH ON CH4 FB!!!
Bzzz
FIVE MILLION VIEWS! GET IN!

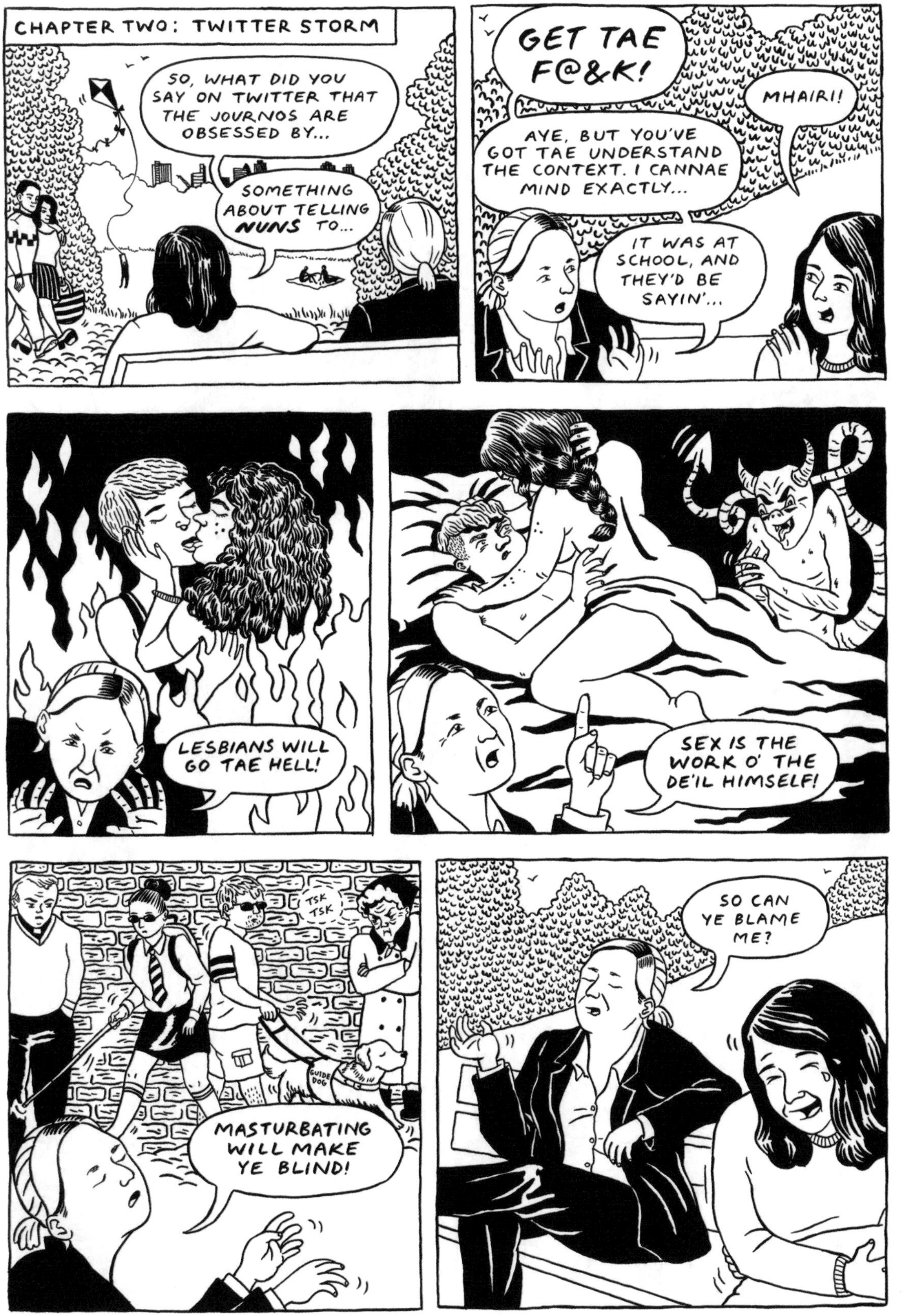
CHAPTER TWO: TWITTER STORM
SO, WHAT DID YOU SAY ON TWITTER THAT THE JOURNOS ARE OBSESSED BY...
SOMETHING ABOUT TELLING NUNS TO...
GET TAE F@&K!
MHAIRI!
AYE, BUT YOU'VE GOT TAE UNDERSTAND THE CONTEXT. I CANNAE MIND EXACTLY...
IT WAS AT SCHOOL, AND THEY'D BE SAYIN'...
LESBIANS WILL GO TAE HELL!
SEX IS THE WORK O' THE DE'IL HIMSELF!
TSK TSK
GUIDE DOG
MASTURBATING WILL MAKE YE BLIND!
SO CAN YE BLAME ME?

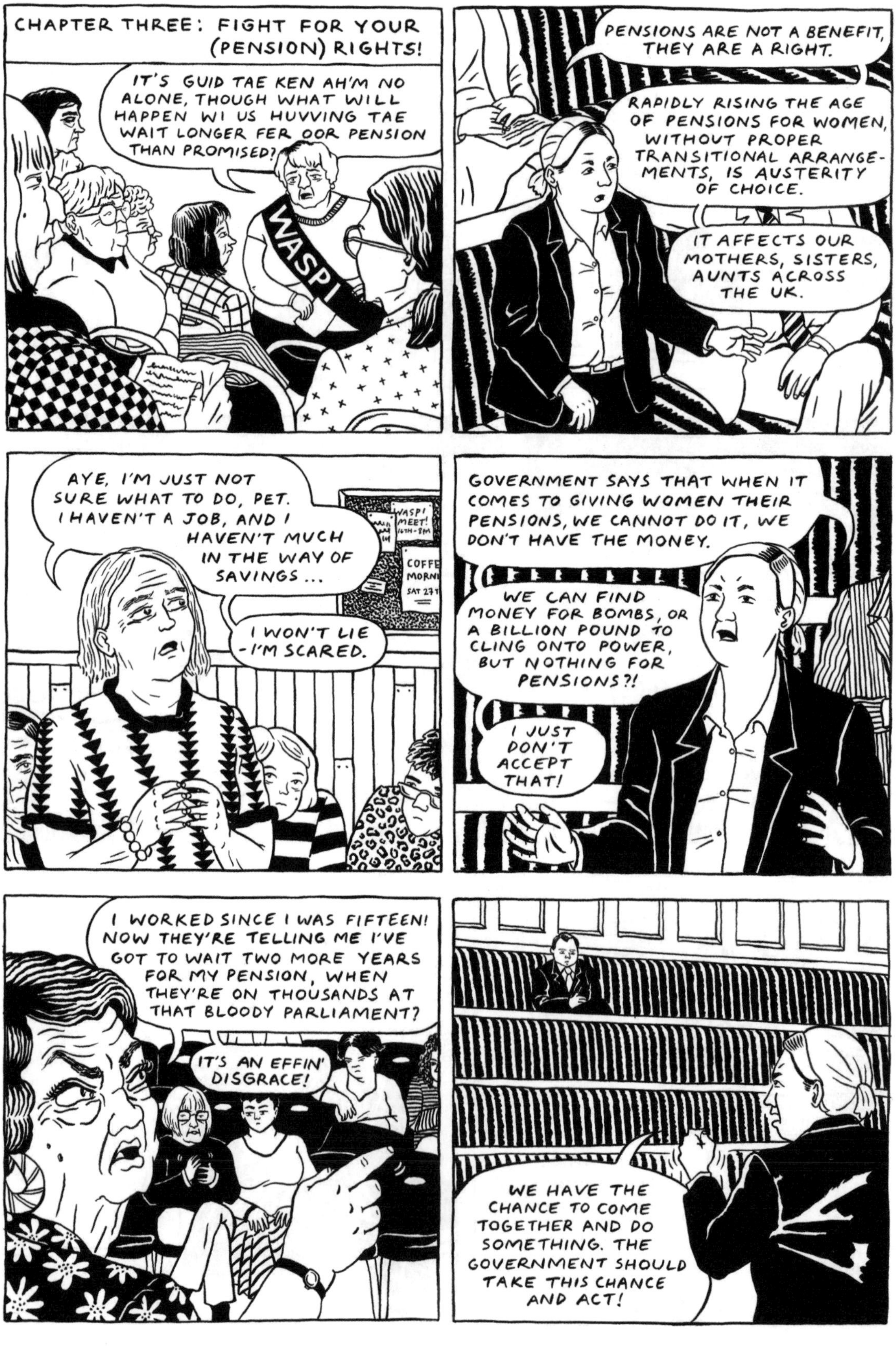
CHAPTER THREE: FIGHT FOR YOUR (PENSION) RIGHTS!
IT'S GUID TAE KEN AH'M NO ALONE, THOUGH WHAT WILL HAPPEN WI US HUVVING TAE WAIT LONGER FER OOR PENSION THAN PROMISED?
WASPI
PENSIONS ARE NOT A BENEFIT, THEY ARE A RIGHT.
RAPIDLY RISING THE AGE OF PENSIONS FOR WOMEN, WITHOUT PROPER TRANSITIONAL ARRANGE-MENTS, IS AUSTERITY OF CHOICE.
IT AFFECTS OUR MOTHERS, SISTERS, AUNTS ACROSS THE UK.
AYE, I'M JUST NOT SURE WHAT TO DO, PET. I HAVEN'T A JOB, AND I HAVEN'T MUCH IN THE WAY OF SAVINGS...
I WON'T LIE - I'M SCARED.
WASPI MEET!
GOVERNMENT SAYS THAT WHEN IT COMES TO GIVING WOMEN THEIR PENSIONS, WE CANNOT DO IT, WE DON'T HAVE THE MONEY.
WE CAN FIND MONEY FOR BOMBS, OR A BILLION POUND TO CLING ONTO POWER, BUT NOTHING FOR PENSIONS?!
I JUST DON'T ACCEPT THAT!
I WORKED SINCE I WAS FIFTEEN! NOW THEY'RE TELLING ME I'VE GOT TO WAIT TWO MORE YEARS FOR MY PENSION, WHEN THEY'RE ON THOUSANDS AT THAT BLOODY PARLIAMENT?
IT'S AN EFFIN' DISGRACE!
WE HAVE THE CHANCE TO COME TOGETHER AND DO SOMETHING. THE GOVERNMENT SHOULD TAKE THIS CHANCE AND ACT!

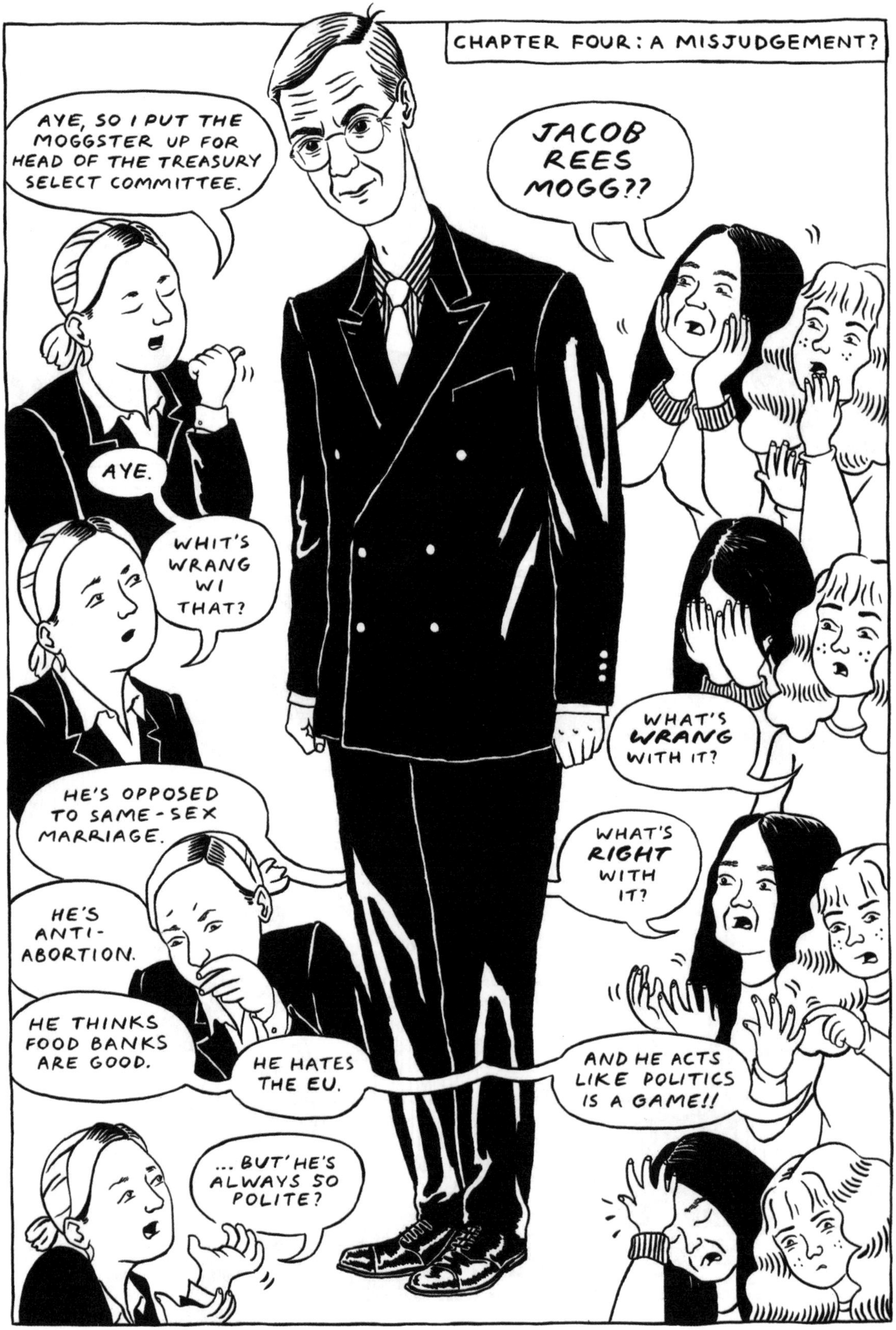
CHAPTER FOUR: A MISJUDGEMENT?
AYE, SO I PUT THE MOGGSTER UP FOR HEAD OF THE TREASURY SELECT COMMITTEE.
JACOB REES MOGG??
AYE.
WHIT'S WRANG WI THAT?
WHAT'S WRANG WITH IT?
HE'S OPPOSED TO SAME-SEX MARRIAGE.
WHAT'S RIGHT WITH IT?
HE'S ANTI-ABORTION.
HE THINKS FOOD BANKS ARE GOOD.
HE HATES THE EU.
AND HE ACTS LIKE POLITICS IS A GAME!!
... BUT HE'S ALWAYS SO POLITE?

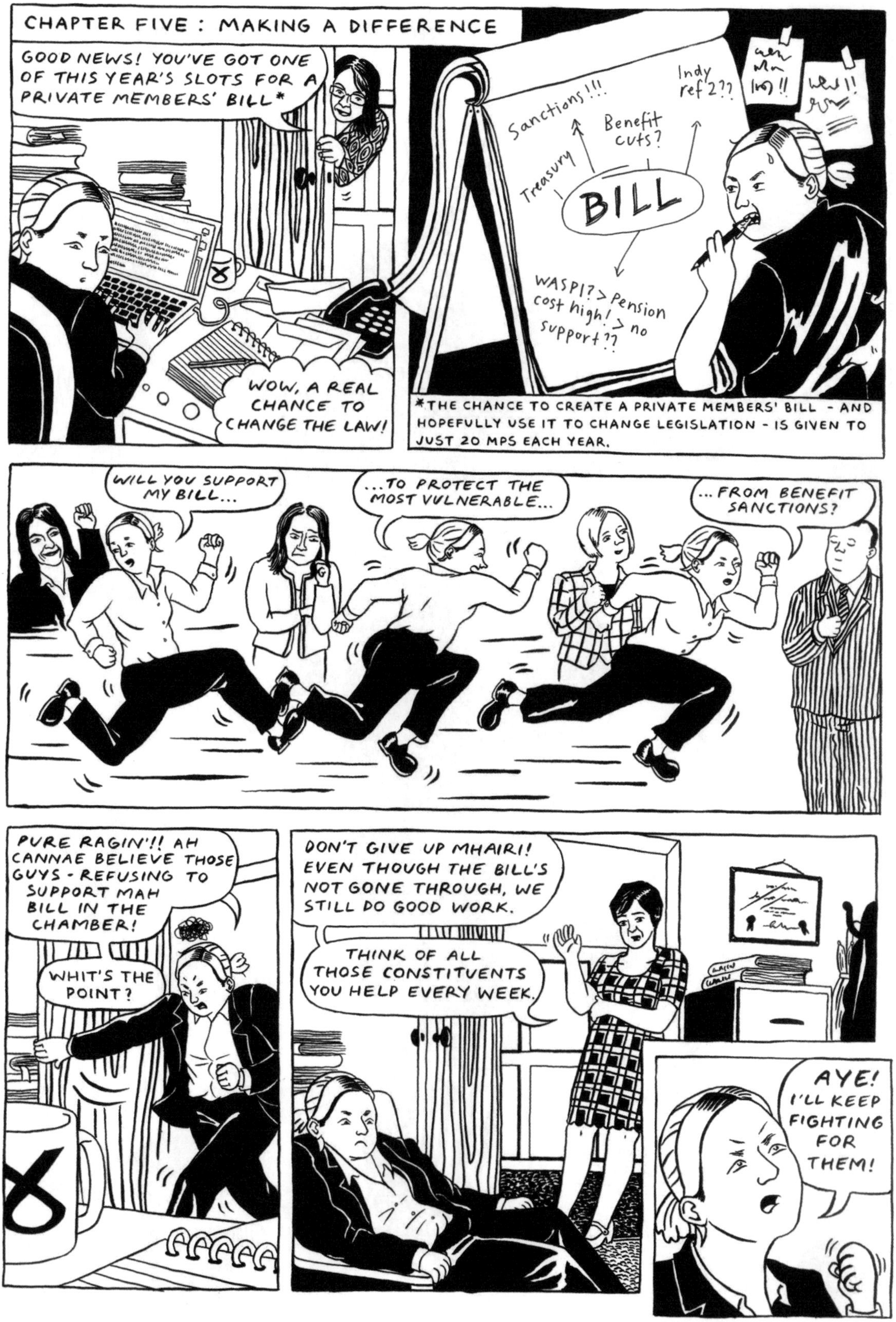
CHAPTER FIVE : MAKING A DIFFERENCE
GOOD NEWS! YOU'VE GOT ONE OF THIS YEAR'S SLOTS FOR A PRIVATE MEMBERS' BILL*
WOW, A REAL CHANCE TO CHANGE THE LAW!
BILL
Treasury
Sanctions!!!
Benefit cuts?
Indy ref 2??
WASPI? > Pension cost high! > no support??
*THE CHANCE TO CREATE A PRIVATE MEMBERS' BILL - AND HOPEFULLY USE IT TO CHANGE LEGISLATION - IS GIVEN TO JUST 20 MPS EACH YEAR.
WILL YOU SUPPORT MY BILL...
...TO PROTECT THE MOST VULNERABLE...
...FROM BENEFIT SANCTIONS?
PURE RAGIN'!! AH CANNAE BELIEVE THOSE GUYS - REFUSING TO SUPPORT MAH BILL IN THE CHAMBER!
WHIT'S THE POINT?
DON'T GIVE UP MHAIRI! EVEN THOUGH THE BILL'S NOT GONE THROUGH, WE STILL DO GOOD WORK.
THINK OF ALL THOSE CONSTITUENTS YOU HELP EVERY WEEK.
AYE! I'LL KEEP FIGHTING FOR THEM!

We'd like to thank all the contributors to the We Shall Fight Until We Win Kickstarter, who made this book possible.

@kayjoon
Abbie Urquhart
Adele Forbes
Adiba Jaigirdar
Ailie Crerar
Al, Lachlan, and Katie Sharp
Alex Burton-Keeble
Alex Peterson
Alexis B
Ali Frost
Ali Grotkowski
Ali Webster (TnSMOM)
Alison Savage
Alison Storm Misché
Alistair Canlin
Allan MacRitchie
Ally Shwed
Aly Pavitt
Amelia Simpson
Amie Jordan
Amita Sandya Ganesh
Ana Delia Sotelo Molero
Andréa Fernandes
Andrew Sharp
andykisaragi
Ania Campbell
Anna Larson
Anne Marie Mackin
Aoife Deery
Aoife Kuo
Ariana
Arusa Qureshi
Ashley Orndorff
Avon Ewens
Barbara Aubrey
Bec Sanderson
Becca Day-Preston
Becki Cardosi
Benjamin Bisset
Bethany Duck
Bex Hughes
Billy Rumbold
Blanca Porta
Bobbi Boyd
Brandon D'Orlando
Briony Cullin
Bryony Cole
Cadence Chance
Cai Wilkinson
Caitrin Armstrong
Cameron Foster
Cara Stasick
Cara Viola
Carla Gottschald Chiodi
Carleen Boer
Carly Anne Jerome
Caro Clarke
Caroline Campbell
Caroline O'Brien

Carolyn Black
Carolyn Rae
Catherine Berry
Catherine Desia Bolt
Catherine Maddox
Catriona Cox
Charles Craddock
Charley Hemmings
Charlotte Brady
Chelsea Chadwick
Chiara Mac Call
Chris Boyce-Butler
Chris McQueer
Christina & Rachel A'Hara
Christina Neuwirth
Christina Parsons Smith
Christine Cebulski Evans
Cia Jackson
CJ Cook
Claire Dean
Claire Park
Claire Squires
Claire Withers
Clare Fairbairn
Clare Owen
Claudia Esteves
Clémence Moulaert
Clydebank High School
Cole Henley
Colin Bell
Colm Currie
Comichaus
Craig Hanlon
Craig M Shaw
Crystal F
D Franklin
Dagmar Baumann
Daiden O'Regan
Daisy Carnegie
Dan Whitehead
Danielle Wilson
Daphne van de Burgwal
Darla Louisa Blakiston Moore
Dave Coates
Dave Cook
Dave Fraser
David Chang
David Lars Chamberlain
David MacDonald Graham
Debbie Jenkinson
Deborah Preuss
Dennis Riethmüller
Diane Stewart
Dragon Sexmaster
Eilidh Porrelli
Eleanor Smith
Elena Soper
Elise & Christoffer
Elizabeth Cathcart

Elizabeth Duggan
Elizabeth Evatt
Elizabeth Jackson
Elizabeth King
Elizabeth Smith
Elizabeth Stanley
Elizabeth Wynn
Ellen Power
Ellen Simpson
Ellis Griffiths
Emily and Rebecca Strong
Emily B. Owen
Emily Henderson
Emily Oram
Emily Parry
Emily Zinkin
Emma Varney
Emporium Purgatorio
Erin Lux
Erin Subramanian
Estelle Tidey
Esther Sparrow
Ever Dundas
Everest Madelyn Chua
F. E. Clark
Fabiana B Romero
Family Blorge
Family Sharp
Felipe Bustos Sierra
Fenric Cayne
Fermin Serena Hortas
Finbarr Farragher
Fiona Ashley
Fiona Cochrane
For Ruby-Rose Brown
Francis Mckee
Fraser Campbell
Fred McNamara
Freiya
Garry Mac
Gary Kaill
Gavin Wilson
Georgie Aldridge
Gillian Hunt
Gio Guimarães
Giulia Carla Rossi
G-Man (Comics Anonymous)
GMarkC
Gordon Mclean
Grace Rose
Graeme Macrae Burnet
Grainne McEntee
Hafsa Alkhudairi
Hannah Cook
Hannah Maguire
Hannah McGeechan
Hannah Sheehy
Hattie Kennedy
Helen Govier

Helen MacDonald
Howard Kistler
Iain S Ross
Imogen Louise Wilson
Ingrid Clouston
Irene Almazán
Isaac 'Will It Work' Dansicker
Isabelle Erbacher
Isobel Dew
J
Jack Davies
Jade Esson
James Corcoran
James MacKinnon
Jamie Chazen
Jamie Norman
Jane Hanmer
Jane LDS
Janice Weir
Janina Birtolo
Janine Mahalick
Jen Harris
Jenna Robertson
Jenni Nock
Jennifer D Gies
Jess aka Loadofolbobbins
Jess Glaisher
Jess Watkins
Jessica Jones
Jessica Kimelman
Jessica Rose Sharp
Jim Moore
Jo Sharp
Joanna Evans Cohen
João Sobral
John MacLeod
Jon Peer
Jon Y
Jonathan Schäfer and Graeme Lyon
José Carlos Rodríguez
Jude LJ Bellingham
Julie Cheung
Juliet Robinson
Katherine Blackburn
Katherine E. Knotts
Kathleen Reed
Kathleen Szczyry
Katie Careless
Katie Lumsden
Katie Whittle
Katie Young
Kelvin Smith
Kerry McShane
KET Strait
Kevin Addies
Kiley Pole
Kim Kelly
Kimberly Cincilla

Kimberly M. Lowe
Kirsten Murray
Kirsten Wilson
Kirsty Connell-Skinner
Kirsty Mackay
Kirsty Marie McNeill
Klas Rönnbäck
Knittingmayhem
Kovács Róbert Dániel
kristin walter
Kristy Diaz
Krisztián Tóth
Laila Riakos
Lara Kipp
Lara Townsend
Laura Brevitz
Laura Carberry
Laura Clements
Laura Frame
Laura James
Laura Locke
Laura Pietrobon and Ellie
Dunbar
Laura Sheach
Laura Waddell
Lauren Doogan
Lauren McKay
Laurie J. Burkland
Lavinia Sonnenberg
Lea Intelmann
Lea Mara
Leah Bevan-Haines
Leah McDowell
Leila Fouda
Leonie Duane
Lesley Macniven
Lesley Mitchell
Lily Shirres
Linsay Halladay
Lisa Donoghue
Lisa McCurrach
Lise Tannahill
Liz M Parr
Lizzie Huxley-Jones
Loïs A Wolffe
Louise Corcoran
Louise Fairbairn
Louise Thompson
Lucie Santos
Lucky Target Comics
Lynlee Howard-Payne
M J Dobney
MA Creative Writing @
EdinburghNapier
Madeline Adeane
Mairi Claire Hubbard
Mairi McKay
Marc Standaert
Maria Ehmann
María Eugenia Reimunde
Marianne MacRae
Marie-Anne Dentzer

Mark A. Held
Mark Bolsover
Marlen Beckmann
Marta and Serena Venturu
Mary Hanora O'Sullivan
Mary Paulson-Ellis
Mary Young
Mathias F
Mathias Kollmitzer
Matilda Marsden
Matt Kund
Matt Macdonald
Meagan Lois Tanti
Meggie Sherriffs
Melissa & Gaia Hampson-
Smith MJHScontemporary
Mer Spinosa
Michael Park
Mika Cook
Mike Murphy
Mike Stock
Monty Nero
Morven Gow
Muireann Crowley
Murray Robertson
Nadine Aisha Jassat
Naomi Frisby
Naomi Newman
Natalia Figueroa
Natalie Ohlson
Natasha R. Chisdes
Nathaniel Kunitsky
Nicholas George
Nick Kirkman
Nick Lowry
Nick Mellish
Nicola West
Nicole Brandon
Nikki Bi
Nina and Grace Norris
Noel Johnson
Noelle Harrison
Oddvar Løvås
P Cochrane
Pablo Perez Ruiz
Paige Kimble
Patricia Davis
Paul Bristow
Paul McAnaney
Paul Rutherford
Paul Whelan
Paula Z
Pax Lowey
Peggy Hughes
Peter LaPrade
Peter Lynch
Petra Pavlikova
Philip Leith
Philip Wilson
PJ Anderson
Polly Rae Keery
Rachael North

Rachel Alexander
Rachel Davies
Rachel F Smith
Rachel H Sanders
Rachel M. Delisle
Rachel Mann
Raisa Hassan
Rebecca Abts Wright
Rebecca Fraser
Rebecca Horner
Rebecca Mutton
Ren Aldridge
Rhys Owain Williams
Richard Wainman
Ricky Monahan Brown
Rob Giddings
Robert Macmillan
Robin Jones
Rog Harrison
Rosalind Gibb
Rosie McKean
Ross McCleary
Ross McDonald
Rowena McIntosh
Ruby Jessica Davidson
Russell Barker
Russell Moran
Ruth Boreham
Ruth Ellis
Ruth Lillian Foulis
Ryan R. Snyder
Sally A Morrow
Samantha Barr
Sara Hunt
Sara Lisa Bard
Sara O'Connor
Sarah Aeschbacher
Sarah Artt
Sarah Cameron
Sarah Clarkson
Sarah E M Mason
Sarah Emery
Sarah Garnham
Sarah Glerup
Sarah J. Burgess
Sarah Pybus
Sarah Rose
Scots Whay Hae!
Sean Patrick Foley
ShadowCub
Sharon Bussey-Reschka
Sharon Rhys-Davies
Shaun Manning
Sheena Semple
Shelley J. Anderson
Shona Thoma
Simon Cree
Simone Kassel
Siobhan Dunlop
Siobhan Shields
Sofía Fernández Becerra
Song, by Toad

Sophie
Sophie Waddy
Steve Nicoll
Steve Tanner
Steven Dawson
Steven Fraser
Steven Ingram
Stevie Williams
Stuart Cruickshank
Stuart Kenny
Sue Dowling
Suman Bajwa
Susan Gilbert
Susie McIvor
Suzie Duncan-Bendix
Suzy Fuldale
Svend Andersen
Tamsin L. Grainger
Tasha Turner
The FE Doran Centre
Thomas H. Brand
Thomas MIGLINCI
Thomas Welsh
Timothy C. Baker
Timothy J. Berg
Tom Farrington
Tonje Hefte
Vex Batchelder
Viccy Adams
Vicki Jarrett
Vicky Ingram
Vince Hunt
Vincent AxeVince Hubau
Virginia Riches
Wanda Caulfield
Will C.
Will McInnes
William McDaid
Yasmin Sulaiman
Yvonne T Bolton
Zelda Doyle
Zhané Storm Moledina
Zoe Anne Young Flatman
Zoe MacLeod
Zoe Mitchell
Zoe Murphy